GW00391476

GOOD HOUSEKEEPING

Planning a
Wedding

PRACTICAL LIBRARY

GH

GOOD HOUSEKEEPING

Planning a Wedding

The comprehensive guide to:

- *Choosing the perfect dress*
- *Arranging the reception*
- *Organising music, transport, flowers, photographers*
- *Booking the ceremony and inviting guests*

PLUS Answers to all the
confusing etiquette questions

EBURY PRESS LONDON

Published by Ebury Press
An imprint of The Random Century Group
Random Century House
20 Vauxhall Bridge Road, London SW1V 2SA

First impression 1990

Copyright © 1990 The Random Century Group

All rights reserved. No part of this publication may be reproduced,
stored in a retrieval system, or transmitted in any form or by any
means, electronic, mechanical, photocopying, recording or
otherwise, without the prior permission of the copyright owner.

The expression GOOD HOUSEKEEPING as used in the title of this
book is the trade mark of The National Magazine Company Ltd
and The Hearst Corporation, registered in the United Kingdom
and USA, and other principal countries of the world, and is the
absolute property of The National Magazine Company Ltd and
The Hearst Corporation. The use of this trade mark other than with
the express permission of The National Magazine Company Ltd or
The Hearst Corporation is strictly prohibited.

Cover design by Roger Hammond

British Library Cataloguing in Publication Data
Arnold, Jane
    Planning a wedding. – (Good housekeeping
    practical library).
    1. Weddings. Planning
I. Title
395'.22

ISBN 0 85223 866 5

Filmset in Palatino by Textype Typesetters, Cambridge
Printed and bound in Great Britain by Mackays of Chatham PLC,
Chatham, Kent

Contents

Introduction

Weddings are the stuff that dreams – as well as photographs – are made of. But a really memorable wedding is the result of careful planning, and this takes time and plenty of effort. This book will help you to organise all the elements of the wedding you choose.

Many questions pose themselves about the conventions and etiquette of a wedding: after all, this is the first and only time most people need such information. Who has to make a speech? What does the best man do? How long should the reception last? What happens at the ceremony itself? You'll find the answers to these and numerous other questions here, as well as advice on choosing what to wear, compiling your guest list, selecting appropriate music, hiring cars, videos and photographs, choosing flowers, and organising the reception.

There are checklists in each section, so you can keep track of your progress, and suggestions about where to go to buy or hire everything you need. At the end of this book is a thought-provoking section on starting a new life together, with all the decisions and adjustments that this involves.

Planning your wedding may be hard work, but it is also great fun. And at the end of all the preparations you can relax, confident that everything will run smoothly, and can thoroughly enjoy yourselves on the exciting first day of your new life together.

1

Announcing the Engagement

Your engagement is the formal announcement of your intention to marry. Proposals of marriage take many forms, and the length of an engagement can vary enormously, but getting engaged is when you publicly declare your plans. The first people to be let in on your exciting news must be the bride's parents, who should be told as soon as the couple have reached their decision. It's not necessary these days for a man to ask permission of a woman's father for 'her hand in marriage', but it makes a lot of sense to get your relationship with your future in-laws off to a good start.

If the bride no longer lives with her parents, you should try to visit them together to tell them your news. Don't do it over the phone or by letter unless distance makes a personal meeting impossible. Although these things are far less formal nowadays than they were in the past, it is not unreasonable for the bride's parents to want to be reassured that their daughter is making a good choice and to welcome their future son-in-law into the family. This will also be your first chance to discuss all the plans that have to be made for the wedding.

Once you have told the groom's parents, it is a good idea to arrange for the two sets of parents to meet, so that they can get to know each other before the wedding.

You will also want to put your other relatives and close friends in the picture as soon as possible, either in person or by a phone call, or a short note.

Newspaper notices

You may want to put an announcement in a local or national paper to tell the world about your engagement. The traditional national papers are *The Times* and the *Daily Telegraph*. The notice can be quite brief and the wording straightforward and traditional as in the examples shown. Take a look at the announcements in the newspaper of your choice and borrow the wording, if you are at all uncertain.

Some couples make the announcement in their own names, without mentioning their parents, and this is especially appropriate if it is a second marriage for either partner. Do mention the date of the wedding, if it has been settled, as shown in the third example. In the fourth example, the bride's parents are divorced.

FORTHCOMING MARRIAGES

Mr M J Reynolds and Miss S West
The engagement is announced between Michael John, youngest son of Mr and Mrs Peter Reynolds of Rochester, Kent, and Sarah, only daughter of Mr and Mrs David West of Guildford, Surrey.

Mr J A Thompson and Miss H J Spencer
The engagement is announced between James Andrew, son of the late Mr W S Thompson and Mrs G K Thompson of York, and Helen Julia, elder daughter of Mr and Mrs M P Spencer of Cambridge.

Mr G C Randle and Miss M L Adams
The engagement is announced and the marriage will take place on 15th August in Edinburgh between Graham Charles, son of Mr and Mrs George Randle of Gloucester, and Mary Louise, younger daughter of Mr and Mrs Robert Adams of Edinburgh.

Mr V E Arnold and Miss S K Jason
The engagement is announced between Vincent Edward, son of Mr and Mrs Stanley Arnold of Northampton and Susan Katharine, daughter of Mr Alan Jason of Oxford and Mrs Madeleine Jason of Northampton.

Your engagement ring

It is customary to mark the engagement with a ring. Only rarely is it presented at the time of the proposal, but it is more usual for the couple to choose it together. Diamonds are by far the most popular gem for engagement rings, chosen by nearly three-quarters of brides-to-be. And a traditional solitaire is still the preferred style. Diamonds have a unique clarity and brilliance, catching the light and sparkling with every move of your hand. They are also very durable, being the hardest gem stone, and will keep their 'fire' through all the years ahead.

If you prefer a ring which has a splash of colour, there are several other traditional stones for engagement rings, including sapphires, rubies, topaz and emeralds. These are often set with diamonds. For something more unusual, opals are attractively milky, with hints of rainbow colour.

There are of course dozens of styles to choose from, and designs vary according to the type, size and number of stones, the setting and the shoulders. Shoulders may be plain, diamond cut or hand engraved, set with diamonds or other precious stones, or even pierced to produce a pattern.

You will find a wide choice of modern engagement rings in most high street jewellers. Antique jewellery can have great charm and delicacy, and you will have a wider range of stones to choose from, such as semi-precious amethysts in all shades from palest lilac to deep purple; burgundy red garnets, golden yellow topaz or tiny pearls. Look in antique shops that sell old jewellery.

Another possibility is to have a ring specially made by a professional jeweller, and this will give you a ring which is highly individual, especially if you want something unusual. The only limit is your imagination – and your pocket. The most reliable way of finding a jewellery designer is by word of mouth. Otherwise, look them up in your Yellow Pages and go and see their work before you commit yourself.

When choosing your engagement ring remember that you

will want to wear it all day, every day. Very chunky designs can be awkward if you want to wear gloves in winter. Make sure that the ring does not protrude too much above the finger, or have any sharp edges in the setting that might get caught in clothes. The ring will eventually be worn with a wedding ring, so check that your finger will be comfortable when two rings are in place.

Whether you buy a new or antique ring, do insure it for its full value as soon as you have bought it.

What does your ring mean?

Gem stones have traditional meanings which you might like to keep in mind when making your choice.

Diamonds – innocence, lasting love
Sapphires – wisdom
Rubies – love and contentment
Emeralds – happiness, success in love
Opals – hope
Topaz – fidelity
Garnets – constancy
Amethysts – sincerity
Pearls – health and beauty

The wedding rings

More and more couples exchange rings during the wedding ceremony, instead of a ring being given to the bride alone. To cater for this, many rings are now available in matching pairs, so that you can both wear a ring of the same design. Of course, there's no need to be completely alike – if a bride chooses a very highly patterned ring, her husband may prefer a plain band, or a simpler design.

There are plenty of designs and several metals to choose from. Plain bands come in different weights, widths and shapes. Or you could choose a style with a plain or patterned bevelled edge. Another alternative is the 'Russian wedding ring', three interlinked bands in different shades of gold. Try the ring on with your engagement ring to judge the effect before choosing.

All about gold   Gold is a soft metal, which would not wear well if used in its pure state, as well as being very expensive. It is therefore alloyed with other metals for use in rings. The word 'carat' is used in two different contexts in jewellery. It refers to a weight when used in conjunction with diamonds, but to purity when used in association with gold. Eighteen-carat gold is purer than 9ct gold, but therefore wears less well. Both easily merit the confirmed status symbol of the jewellery trade, the hallmark. White gold is a light-coloured gold, alloyed with silver. Platinum is a hard-wearing silver-coloured metal, more expensive than gold.

Other gifts   If the bridegroom does not plan to wear a wedding ring, the bride might like to buy him a gift such as a watch or cufflinks, to mark the occasion. It is also usual to give small gifts to the bridesmaids, such as earrings, a gold chain or a bracelet or bangle, on the wedding day.

✳ *ENGAGEMENT AND WEDDING RINGS CHECKLIST* ✳

The engagement ring

What is our budget limit?

Will the ring look good with the wedding ring we have in mind?

Is it comfortable and easy to wear all the time?

How do I clean it? (ask your jeweller's advice)

How much should it be insured for?

The wedding ring

Are we both going to have a wedding ring?

What is our budget limit?

Do we want matching rings?

Will the design we have chosen go well with the engagement ring?

How much should the rings be insured for?

Engagement parties

You might choose to have a party to celebrate your engagement. If you do, it should be held as soon as possible after the engagement is announced. You might even decide to make a surprise announcement at the party, in which case it will have to be arranged very speedily before the news leaks out!

An engagement party can take any form, so you can do whatever suits your situation. Informal drinks at your or your parents' home could include family and friends, or you might prefer to go out for a special meal with your family and celebrate with your friends on a separate occasion. A night out at a restaurant or disco would be fun if you are a young crowd. If you want to be more formal, you could consider hiring a hall, arranging for caterers and really going to town. It's entirely up to you, though cost will, of course, be a limiting factor.

You might like to give your ring its first airing at your party, when everyone will be asking to see it in any case.

Whether or not you give a party, you and your fiancé are likely to receive lots of congratulations cards and some engagement presents, and you should send a note of thanks for these from both of you.

2

What Type of Wedding?

The type of wedding you want is something that will have to be discussed early on with the bride's parents, since they traditionally pay for most of it. But the decision about whether to have a religious or a civil ceremony should rest with the couple themselves. Do you want to marry in church or a register office and is there anything to restrict your choice? Do you want a full, formal white wedding with all the trimmings, or would you prefer something more simple and informal? How do you go about arranging the wedding of your choice, and what happens on the day itself?

Marriage and the law

There are strict rules as to whom you may or may not marry, and the law demands that various conditions be fulfilled before a marriage can take place. Both partners must be over 16, and if either of you is under 18, you must obtain the consent of your parents or guardian. However, in Scotland, anyone over 16 can marry, without permission from their parents.

If either of you has been married before, you may not remarry until you have received the divorce decree absolute. Both partners must be acting of their own free will and be of sound mind. And there is a long list of relatives who may not legally marry each other.

If you plan to marry in the Church of England, you must arrange for the banns to be called. These are an announcement of your intention to marry, read in church on three consecutive Sundays shortly before the wedding, in the parishes in which you both live. Banns are not necessary in Scotland, where it may also be possible to be married at a venue other than a church or register office.

If for some reason there is not enough time for the banns to be called, you can apply for a Common Licence, which takes only one day to be issued. Your minister can tell you how to apply but you have to have been resident in the parish for 15 days. In other denominations, it is the local registrar who grants the marriage licence.

Couples who are planning a register office wedding have to sign a declaration that there is no legal reason preventing the marriage. One of the couple must have lived locally for seven days and will have to wait 21 days for a certificate of authority to marry. If you are in a hurry you can apply for a licence to marry instead, in which case one of you must have lived in the district for 15 days before applying, but you need only wait one day for the licence to be issued.

A properly registered person and a number of other witnesses must be present at every marriage; details will differ slightly according to where the marriage takes place. In England and Wales weddings can be held only within authorised buildings, such as a church or register office, with the exception of Jewish and Quaker ceremonies. However the law is freer on this point in Scotland.

If you plan to marry abroad it is essential to find out what the local requirements are. In general, marriages which take place abroad are recognised in British law, as long as they do not contravene any of the basic British regulations which relate to marriage.

Religious wedding or register office?

Your own beliefs should be the main factor which dictates whether or not you wish to have a religious wedding, but there are some other points to bear in mind.

Remarriage If a partner has been widowed, he or she can remarry in church or a register office, with no restrictions. However, if one or both of you is divorced then it may be more difficult to arrange a religious wedding. Some Church of England ministers will marry you in church, but many prefer to bless the marriage after a civil ceremony instead.

16

The blessing service is straightforward, with a reading, some prayers, perhaps a brief address and the blessing itself. It can take place immediately after the civil ceremony or at a later date. Some ministers like to keep blessing ceremonies fairly low key, so do check before you make any firm arrangements.

The Roman Catholic church has more rigid rules about remarriage, and your priest would be able to tell you what is permissible. Nonconformists, Quakers and Jews can usually remarry with a religious ceremony, provided certain conditions are fulfilled.

Mixed marriages If the two of you want a religious wedding, but belong to different churches, there should be no problem if you belong to a Protestant or Nonconformist church, such as the Churches of England, Scotland and Wales; Methodist, United Reform or Baptist.

If one partner is a Catholic, he or she will need permission to enter a 'mixed' marriage and must undertake to continue in the Catholic faith and endeavour to bring up any children of the marriage as Catholics. The priest must be satisfied that the non-Catholic partner fully understands and agrees to this condition before he will conduct the marriage. A Catholic/non-Catholic couple can also marry in a Protestant church, but a special dispensation will have to be obtained from the bishop.

Quakers accept non-members as long as they are sympathetic to the nature of the Quaker marriage. They will be asked to produce two written recommendations from members of the Quaker group.

If a Christian wants to marry a non-Christian, there could well be difficulties. Catholic and Orthodox churches do not allow such marriages, and in other denominations the minister has the right to refuse to marry you if he is not convinced that both of you accept and understand the Christian faith. The Jewish faith does not subscribe to the idea of mixed marriages, and in these cases it would be almost impossible for the couple to have a religious marriage unless the non-

Jewish partner was prepared to convert to the Jewish faith – a lengthy business.

Setting the date

Once you have decided what sort of wedding you want, you can go ahead with the arrangements. If you want to follow convention and marry on a Saturday, you will need to book the church or register office and reception venue well in advance, especially if you want to marry between June and September. You may need to give six months notice or even longer for a summer wedding. Bear in mind too that many register offices are closed on Saturday afternoons, and that Friday is the next most popular day. It is possible to marry in church on other days of the week, although not generally on a Sunday (or a Saturday in the Jewish faith).

Before you settle on a date, make sure that it doesn't coincide with any popular sporting event such as the Wimbledon final, and that none of your friends are planning their own wedding for the same day! The 13th of the month is a good bet for the non-superstitious, as most people avoid it and reception venues, photographers and so on are more likely to be available.

Some ministers prefer not to hold weddings during Lent (the six weeks before Easter) or Advent (the four weeks before Christmas). If you do marry in Lent, you will not be permitted to decorate the church with flowers, nor to have a peal of bells rung as you arrive and leave.

When choosing the time, you may be restricted by other weddings already booked for the same day. But if you do have some choice, work out the best time in conjunction with the type of reception and the time you wish to leave for your honeymoon. The most popular time to marry is 3pm, but that may involve booking a reception venue for the afternoon and evening, since the meal will not be served until around 5pm. If you want to leave for your honeymoon in the late afternoon you could get married between noon and 2pm, in which case you would book the reception venue for the afternoon only and have a late lunch. Whatever you decide, do be generous when planning your timetable: remember that a formal reception and sit-down meal will last for several hours. You also need to allow time for photography after the service and time for guests to travel to the reception.

Religious weddings

Between meeting the minister to book the church and the wedding day itself, you will have one or more other opportunities to meet and discuss things with him. This will enable you to get to know each other, as well as to organize and plan the day thoroughly, so there are no last-minute hitches.

Rehearsals   You'll both feel less nervous about the service if you have had a run-through beforehand. Most ministers will be happy to arrange this for a day or two before the actual wedding. As many members as possible of the wedding party should attend the rehearsal, including the best man, bridesmaids, bride's father and ushers, as well as the couple.

Church of England

If at least one of you has been baptised into the Christian faith, and can satisfy various residential requirements, the arrangements should be straightforward. Make an appointment to see the minister of the church to discuss details of the wedding. He will in any case want to talk to you about the religious significance of your marriage. He can help you choose appropriate hymns and readings and will take you through the words of the service. Details of flowers to decorate the church, the best place for photographs and any rules about confetti or the photographs should also be discussed.

On the day   The ushers should arrive about 45 minutes before the service is due to begin. They should bring with them the printed orders of service and a supply of buttonholes if these are being provided for guests.

As the guests begin to arrive, the ushers should show them to their seats, according to the seating plan (see below). Traditionally, the bride's family and friends sit on the left hand side of the church, the groom's on the right. Parents sit at the front, with other relatives behind them and friends at the back.

The groom and best man should arrive at least 20 minutes before the ceremony begins. The best man should pay any church fees on behalf of the groom and then the pair can pose for photographs before taking their seats in the front right pew to wait for the bride to arrive.

By this time the organist will be playing softly while the guests assemble. The minister will usually arrive 15–20 minutes in advance of the bride.

The car bringing the bridesmaids should arrive about 10 minutes before the ceremony so that they can have photographs taken. The bride's mother, who often travels with the bridesmaids, should be the last person to take her seat, in the front left hand pew. Often a male member of the family will be with her and an usher should escort her personally to her seat. She should leave a place to her right, so that the bride's father can join her when the bride has been given away.

The bride arrives   Last to arrive at the church are the bride and her father, who will pause outside for a few moments to have a photograph taken. The bridesmaids should adjust the bride's veil and train and ensure that she has moved her engagement ring to her right hand so that her left hand is ready to receive the wedding ring.

The bridesmaids and any other attendants then take up their positions behind the bride. The minister can either wait for the bride at the chancel steps, or else meet her at the door, accompanied by the choir if they are singing at the service, and precede her down the aisle.

The organist will start playing the entrance music and the congregation stand. The groom and best man move out of their pew to the chancel steps, and can turn to watch the bride walk slowly down the aisle on her father's right arm.

When the bride arrives at the chancel steps, she is greeted by the groom. She turns and hands her bouquet to her chief bridesmaid, who can also help her lift back her veil. If the bride prefers, the veil can be left in place until the register is signed. The minister can then say a few introductory words to the congregation and a hymn is often sung. The marriage ceremony can then begin.

The ceremony   The exact wording will depend on whether the bride and groom have chosen to use the 1662 authorised Prayer Book, or the updated version. The 1662 version used more poetic, archaic language such as 'With this ring I thee wed', and includes the words 'To love, cherish and to obey.' The 1980 Alternative Service Book uses more direct language, and the vow of obedience is optional.

The service begins with a few words from the minister on the significance of marriage and some advice on the correct approach to marriage. The minister outlines the purposes of marriage and then asks if anyone present knows of any reason why the couple should not be married and gives a last chance for objections to be raised.

The couple are then asked in turn if each will marry the other, and they answer: '*I will*'.

The minister asks who gives the woman to be married. The bride's father should say nothing in reply, but take his daughter's right hand and offer it to the minister, who takes it and places it in the groom's right hand. This concludes the role of the bride's father, and he should step back and take his seat, next to his wife.

The couple then take their wedding vows, in turn, repeating the words after the minister (taken from the 1928 revised version of the 1662 Book of Common Prayer): to you. '*I (name) take thee (name) to my wedded wife/husband, to have and to hold from this day forward, for better for worse; for richer for poorer; in sickness and in health; to love and to cherish; till death us do part, according to God's holy law; and thereto I give thee my troth.*'

The next step is the giving or exchanging of rings. The best man gives the rings to the minister to be blessed. The bride's ring is then given to the groom, who places it on the third finger of her left hand and repeats the words: '*With this ring I thee wed; with my body I thee honour; and all my worldly goods with thee I share. In the name of the Father, the Son and of the Holy Ghost.*' The bride then repeats the same words as she places a ring on her groom's finger.

The minister declares that the couple are now husband and wife, with these words: '*Those whom God has joined together, let no man put asunder.*' The ceremony continues with more hymns, prayers and a short address.

The final stage is to sign the register, which usually takes place in the vestry with the couple, their parents and the best man and attendants present. A copy of the register entry, paid for by the groom, is usually given to the bride by the minister for her to keep.

Leaving the church The party then leaves the church, bride and groom leading the way, to the accompaniment of the organ playing the recessional music. They are followed by chief bridesmaid and best man, any other attendants and the couple's parents, the bride's mother walking with the groom's father and the groom's mother with the bride's father. The congregation follow when the wedding party has passed by.

Other religions

Other denominations differ from the Church of England service in some respects.

Nonconformist or Free Churches The formalities and the service are similar to those of the Church of England, although there is no need for banns to be called and a registrar may have to be present. The order of service and wording may be slightly altered.

Roman Catholic Church Both partners will need to visit the priest several months before the wedding to receive instruction, complete paperwork and possibly arrange for a registrar to be present. Marriage is usually celebrated with the Nuptial Mass, where bride and groom can take communion together. The ceremony begins with prayers and the Act of Penance. Bible and Liturgical readings follow before the actual marriage takes place. The couple make their vows and declare their consent before exchanging rings. More prayers and the Creed are said before the signing of the register. The Mass, if celebrated, follows, and the service ends with a blessing.

Jewish weddings Both partners must apply for the chief rabbi's authorisation and various documents and witnesses will need to be organised. Usually the wedding will take place in a synagogue, but it can be held elsewhere as long as it still takes place under a *chuppah* (wedding canopy). Bride and groom are expected to fast on the day of the wedding until the ceremony is over.

The groom arrives first and sits with his father and best man in the Warden's box. When the ceremony begins he stands under the *chuppah*. The bride usually comes in with her father, although she may be accompanied instead by her mother and future mother-in-law. The bridesmaids follow.

The groom is asked by the minister to approve the witnesses and agree to undertake various basic obligations to his wife. The bride then steps under the *chuppah* and stands beside the groom and the marriage takes place.

Quakers Application must be made at least six weeks before the date of the wedding. There is some paperwork to be completed, which the registering officer of the Monthly Meeting can deal with. The marriage is very simple and is held at a meeting for worship, before the assembled Friends.

Register office weddings

Although register office weddings are shorter than church ceremonies, they can still have a dignity and formality of their own. First the registrar explains the proceedings to the couple on their own and this is when the fees are paid. The guests then come in for the ceremony itself.

The registrar gives a short address to the assembled company before the marriage takes place, then the couple and their two witnesses sign the register.

Photography is not usually allowed during the ceremony, but you can often pose for some pictures in the register office afterwards and more photographs are usually taken outside, or on the steps of, the register office.

∗ WEDDING DAY CHECKLIST ∗

Keep this list handy on the big day as a memory-jogger

Time of hairdresser's appointment

Have the flowers arrived?

Has the cake been delivered to the reception?

Have the bride's luggage and going-away clothes been taken to the reception?

Have the ushers taken the orders of service and buttonholes to church?

Who is looking after the couple's travel documents?

Who is taking care of the wedding clothes after the reception?

What time is the photographer due at the house?

What time are the bridesmaids due to arrive?

Does everyone have the right car keys with them?

When is the first car due?

When is the second car due?

3

Countdown to the Wedding Day

Here are complete checklists of all the arrangements to be made, so that you can keep a note of your progress and ensure that nothing is forgotten. Making the various arrangements shouldn't be all your responsibility, of course. Your parents will take care of some of them, your fiancé others, but it is best that one person keeps an overall check.

As soon as you have set the date

* Decide whether you want to be married in a church or register office.

* Will the wedding be formal or informal?

* Visit the minister who will be conducting the wedding to book the time and date. Do this well in advance, especially if you intend to marry during the summer.

* If you are planning a register office wedding, visit the superintendent registrar to give notice of the marriage. It will take three weeks to receive a certificate of authority to marry, after which the marriage must take place within three months of the date of giving notice.

* Find out if you will need to make any special arrangements regarding a wedding licence, and get these under way.

* Set your budget – discuss with your fiancé and parents.

* Choose and book a reception venue unless you're having the reception at home. It's a good idea to have a meal there first, or look in on another wedding reception before making your final decision.

* Book the caterers if necessary.

* Book the cars to take you to and from the wedding.

* Book the photographer and video, if required.

* Approach your bridesmaids, best man and ushers and make sure they keep the date free.

* Draw up a guest list in consultation with both families.

Three to five months before the wedding

* Decide on your honeymoon destination and make all the necessary bookings.

* Remember to book a hotel room for your wedding night, if necessary.

* Start thinking in detail about your wedding dress and bridesmaids' dresses.

* Discuss your fiancé's outfit. If you want the men in the wedding party to wear formal clothes, make sure that they are all informed in plenty of time so that they can make arrangements to hire their outfits.

* Order the wedding cake.

* For a home-made wedding cake, bake the cakes now and make arrangements for professional icing to be done nearer the time, if necessary.

* Have a second meeting with the minister to discuss the final details of the ceremony. Check whether confetti is permitted in the church grounds.

* Book the bellringers if wanted.

* Book a date and time to rehearse the ceremony shortly before the wedding day.

* Make appointments to see the organist and choir master to discuss the choice of music. If necessary, listen to some tapes or records to help you decide. Once the music has been chosen, you can finalise the wording in the orders of service.

* Book any singers or musicians needed to perform during the ceremony.

* Order the wedding stationery. When calculating, remember that you need one invitation per couple or family, but one order of service per guest. This is the time to order any other items that need to be specially printed: matchbooks, napkins, tablecloths etc.

* Book any entertainment needed for the reception and confirm all details in writing.

Two months before the wedding

* Send out the invitations (do this at least six weeks before the wedding).
* Make out a detailed wedding present list to send to guests, or place your list with the store of your choice.
* Buy your wedding rings.
* Buy any gifts you plan to give to your attendants or parents.
* Buy any special wedding gifts for each other.
* Make sure that your wedding clothes will be ready in time.
* Buy your going-away outfit and any clothes you will need for your honeymoon.
* Have another meeting with the vicar to arrange for the banns to be read.
* Order bouquets for yourself and attendants; buttonholes for the men in the wedding party and guests; corsages for the bride's and groom's mothers.
* Organise details of floral arrangements for ceremony and reception and order any flowers needed.
* Have a meeting with your caterers and choose the food and wine for the reception.
* If you are preparing the food for your own reception, make a detailed list and start cooking items that can be frozen.
* Buy shoes and underwear to complete your wedding and going-away outfits.
* Make sure your passport is up to date and change your name in it if you wish (forms to do this are available at your Post Office, but allow at least six weeks for the new passport to come through).
* Arrange any injections necessary for your honeymoon. Ask your doctor if any of the injections have side-effects and if necessary arrange an appointment for a day when you are not too busy.
* Make an appointment to visit your family planning clinic if necessary.

Four to six weeks before the wedding

✳ Keep a careful record of invitation acceptances and refusals as they come in.

✳ Send a copy of your wedding present list to any guest who requests one.

✳ Work out the number of people to whom you will be sending pieces of cake after the wedding, and order boxes from a stationer.

✳ Take your headdress along to the hairdresser to discuss a suitable style, have a trial run if necessary, and make an appointment for the day.

✳ Make sure that your wedding dress fits perfectly and that you are happy with it. Try it on with the underwear and shoes you intend to wear on the day.

✳ Have a session with your attendants to make sure there are no problems with any of their outfits.

✳ Book any beauty treatments you plan to have before the wedding.

✳ Check that your fiancé has made all the necessary arrangements for his clothes, the honeymoon, etc.

✳ Arrange for your name to be changed on bank accounts, building society passbooks, tax records, driving licence, doctor's records etc.

✳ Submit wording to your local paper if you want them to carry an announcement of the wedding.

✳ Write thank-you notes for wedding presents promptly, as you receive them.

Two weeks before the wedding

✳ Make a final count of the number of guests who are expected to attend the reception and confirm the number in writing to the caterers.

✳ Make out a seating plan for the reception if needed. Write out place cards if necessary.

✳ Check that the bride's father, groom and best man have prepared their speeches.

* Order foreign currency or traveller's cheques for your honeymoon.
* Make a final confirmation of all arrangements: florist, photographer, video, cars, reception, cake, church details such as choir, bellringers, honeymoon bookings.
* Make arrangements for your stag night/hen party.

One week before the wedding

* Try on your wedding dress and all accessories to make sure everything is comfortable and still fits well.
* Practise your wedding day make-up.
* Try to have a full rehearsal of the ceremony at the church with all the main participants. If you are having any very young attendants, let them go home after they have practised following you down the aisle, otherwise they will tend to get bored or very nervous.
* Time the journey to the church so that you know exactly when you will need to leave home.
* Make sure you have everything you need for the honeymoon. You can finish packing on the night before the wedding if necessary. Double-check any arrangements made to take your case to the reception.
* The day before, make a final double-check of all arrangements – and then try and have an early night!

4

The Best Man and Attendants

If you are getting married in church, your choice of best man and chief bridesmaid can make an important contribution to the smooth running of your wedding. Both should be dependable friends or relations, who can be relied on to give you the support and back-up that you will need. Their traditional duties are listed here, but you may want to ask them to be more – or less – involved, depending on the size of the wedding and the other help you have. Talk it over when you invite them to take part.

You may also want to ask the children in the families to be bridesmaids or page boys. Although tiny children look very appealing in the bridal retinue, do remember that it may be difficult to persuade them to stand still and keep quiet during the ceremony. You will need to have a chief bridesmaid who is confident that she can keep them in control.

You will also need one or two ushers. Although ushers have less responsibility than the best man, you should still pick male friends or relatives who you know to be reliable.

The best man

He is usually the brother or best friend of the groom. His job is not only to give practical help, both before the wedding and on the day itself, but to organise the groom and help calm his inevitable nerves. He has certain responsibilities on the day.

The best man's duties

✳ It is the best man's responsibility to see that the groom gets home safely after a stag night party and is in a fit state for the wedding! For this reason, it's a very good idea to fix the stag night for a date earlier in the preceding week, rather than on the eve of the big day.

✳ Organises the ushers at the church.

* Checks that buttonholes have been ordered and will be at the church.
* Makes sure orders of service are at the church to be distributed to guests by the ushers.
* Ensures that both he and the groom have the appropriate clothes, ready in time for the big day.
* Arranges for the bride's and groom's honeymoon luggage to be taken to the reception venue. If the couple are staying at a hotel locally overnight, the luggage may be taken there instead.
* Keeps the rings safe and accessible until needed during the ceremony.
* Gives the groom moral support before the wedding and makes sure he gets to the church in plenty of time. Sits with the groom until the bride arrives.
* Arranges transport for himself from church to reception.
* Witnesses the signing of the register.
* Accompanies the chief bridesmaid out of the church.
* Is the last to leave for the reception, having made sure that all the guests have transport.
* Pays any church fees on the day, on behalf of the groom.
* Makes sure that a car is available to take the couple away from the reception. This might involve arranging a taxi or hire car (confirm booking on the day before); ensuring that the groom's own car is at the reception venue on the day; or organising for a non-drinking friend to drive the couple to their destination.
* Takes care of the groom's travel documents until needed.
* May take part in the receiving line at the reception.
* Makes a speech at the reception, replying to the toast to the bridesmaids.
* Reads out any Telemessages or cards, vetting them first for any unsuitable comments.
* May act as master of ceremonies at the reception: introduces speeches, toasts and cake-cutting, announces couple's departure.
* Takes charge of the groom's wedding clothes after the

reception. If these are hired, returns them promptly to the hire company.

The ushers

You can have one or two ushers (or more, for a really big wedding). They act as helpers to the best man, and it is up to him to make sure that they know what to do. Together they should go through the seating arrangements at the church, before the day, so that the ushers can direct guests to their places with the minimum of fuss.

The ushers' duties

✳ Direct guests to their places in church. The ushers should ask guests whether they are friends of the bride or groom, before showing them to a pew on the appropriate side of the church (see seating plan on page 20). Friends of the couple could be directed to either side, preferably the emptier one.
✳ Distribute orders of service or hymn books to guests, and make sure that there is a supply at the front of the church for the wedding party and minister to use.
✳ Show the bride's mother to her seat.
✳ Escort the bridesmaids from the church.
✳ Help the best man to arrange transport for all the guests to the reception.

The bridesmaids and pages

The smaller bridesmaids and page boys are not called on to do much other than look decorative and follow the bride down the aisle. If they are very tiny, then it is part of the chief bridesmaid's job to keep them in order in church.

Usually the smallest bridesmaids walk directly behind the bride, with the chief bridesmaid at the back of the procession. She can step forward momentarily at the chancel steps to take the bouquet from the bride, and to help her lift back her veil if necessary.

Some brides choose to have one small attendant as a flower girl, in which case she may be dressed differently from the other attendants. Her job is to carry a small basket of confetti or petals, and to precede the bride out of the church, scattering petals in her path. It's a very pretty idea, but do check with the church first, to see that there is no objection to the sweeping up that will have to be done afterwards.

The chief bridesmaid is usually a close female relative or friend of the bride. If she is a married woman, then she is known as the matron of honour.

The chief bridemaid's duties

* May help the bride to choose her wedding dress and going-away outfit.
* May also be involved in the choice of dresses for the bridesmaids.
* Arranges a 'hen night' for the bride and other female friends. This is the women's equivalent of the stag night, and again is best several days before the wedding.
* Arrives at the bride's home early on the day and helps the bride to dress.
* Checks that the bride has packed everything she will need for going away, and that the luggage has been sent to the reception.
* Takes charge of the younger bridesmaids, sees that they have their posies, etc, and makes sure they know what to do at the church.
* Arrives at the church before the bride and arranges the bride's dress and veil before they enter the church.
* Takes the bouquet during the ceremony.
* May help the bride lift back her veil.
* Witnesses the signing of the register.
* Leaves the church with the best man.
* The chief bridesmaid (or the bride's mother) can carry a make-up kit for the bride, and supplies for emergency repairs – safety pins, needle and thread, spare tights, tissues, etc.
* Keeps an eye on the young bridesmaids at the reception.
* Helps the bride to change out of her wedding dress and get ready to leave the reception.

5

Your Wedding Guests

Guest lists have a habit of growing to unmanageable and uneconomic proportions! It's important to make sure that all the people you especially want to be at your wedding are invited, but at the same time you don't want to ruffle any family feathers by leaving anyone out. The deciding factor will be your budget for the reception or, if money is no object, practical considerations about how many people the church, register office or the reception venue will comfortably hold.

Who shall we ask?

The best way to tackle the task is for the two of you to sit down – with the bride's parents, if they are paying for the reception – and work out how many people you can afford to invite in order to stay within your budget and still have the kind of reception you want. You will almost inevitably have to do some compromising, especially if you both want to invite a lot of friends.

Decide whether you want couples who have babies or young children to bring them along. Although some people like to have children at the reception, they can be very disruptive during the service itself. Whichever way you decide, you will need to make it quite clear when you send out the individual invitations if children are welcome or not. Do you have any very elderly or handicapped relatives, who may need special help? By all means invite them to share your day, but make sure that someone will be available who is prepared to keep an eye on them and give any assistance needed. If your family is very large – or your budget very small – you could consider having a family-only reception and holding an informal party later on for your friends, to which they might contribute by bringing along food or wine.

Far-flung families may find themselves with guests arriving

Mr and Mrs Michael Spencer
request the pleasure of your company
at the marriage of their daughter
Helen Julia
to
Mr James Thompson
at St Peter's Church, Cambridge
on Saturday 14th August
at 3 o'clock
and afterwards at
The Royal Hotel, Queen Street,
Cambridge

RSVP
10 London Road
Cambridge

Mr and Mrs Michael Spencer
request the pleasure of the company of

....

at the marriage of their daughter
Helen Julia
to
Mr James Thompson
at
St Peter's Church, Cambridge
on
Saturday 14th August
at 3 o'clock
and afterwards at
The Royal Hotel, Queen Street, Cambridge

RSVP
10 London Road
Cambridge

James and Helen
invite

to their marriage
at
St. Peter's Church, Cambridge
on
Saturday 14th August
at
3 o'clock
and afterwards at
the Royal Hotel, Queen Street, Cambridge

~ RSVP ~
10 London Road
Cambridge

from distant parts of the country who will need accommodation for one or more nights. The bride's family may feel unable to cope with visitors on top of all the other arrangements, and if this is the case you should see if anyone else can offer to put people up, or arrange to book your friends or relatives into a hotel or a reliable bed and breakfast.

If one of you has been divorced, it is more considerate to the new partner not to invite members of the ex's family (and almost certainly not the ex in person, no matter how amicable you are). Another potentially tricky area arises when the parents of bride or groom are divorced and one or both of them has remarried. Members of the step-family should be invited, although exactly who receives an invitation will depend to a certain extent on the feelings among the family. The happiest solution is bury any hatchets for the day, invite everyone and rely on them all to behave considerately.

Invitations

Most couples have their invitations specially printed, and large stationers have a selection of styles you can choose from, ranging from very formal to totally untraditional. There are various different wordings to choose from, and some examples are shown on pages 36 and 37.

If the bride's parents are divorced, they may still decide to present a united front for the wedding day, in which case the invitations are worded: *'Mr Alastair Jamieson and Mrs Sheila Jamieson (or Mrs Samuel McKintyre, if the bride's mother has remarried) request the pleasure of your company at the marriage of their daughter...'*

Should one of the bride's parents be dead, invitations come from the surviving parent alone: *'Mrs Mary Tucker requests...'.* In the case of a remarriage of the bride's widowed parent, invitations come from: *'Mr and Mrs Alan Rusbridge request the pleasure of your company at the marriage of his/her daughter...'.* In these circumstances it may ease any confusion if the bride's surname is included on invitations.

Those who are marrying for the second time may want to

send invitations in their own names: *'Mr Tim Buchanan and Miss Rosa Hartley request the pleasure...'*.

The invitations should be sent out at least six weeks before the date of the wedding, so make enquiries at your chosen printer well in advance so that you can order in plenty of time. You will need one invitation for each family, plus a few spares.

It is usual for the bride's mother to send out the invitations, and the groom's mother should supply a list of family members to be invited. Make sure a reply address is included, usually that of the bride's mother. Guests are expected to accept formally, and you should keep a list of acceptances as they start to come in. Use the checklists overleaf to keep the details up to date.

Cancelling or postponing a wedding   There is no need to offer explanations for calling off a wedding. An advertisement can be placed in the press, saying simply: *'The marriage arranged between Mr Simon Webster and Miss Madeleine Walker will not now take place'*, but this is not essential. The parents of the bride should tell close family and friends by phone or letter.

If the wedding is called off when the invitations have already gone out, printed cancellation cards or informal notes should be sent out to all guests. Any gifts that have been received should be returned to the giver, with a brief note of thanks.

Very occasionally a wedding has to be postponed, usually due to the serious illness or death of a close relative. Cards should be sent to the guests, telling them the reason for the postponement and notifying them of the new date if this is known and is not too far hence. The following wording can be used: *'It is deeply regretted that due to the death of Mr Daniel O'Connor the marriage of his daughter Mary to Mr Tim Cunningham on 16 July has been postponed.'*

* GUEST CHECKLIST *

Name and Address	No. in Family	No. of Children	Accepted	Refused

* GUEST CHECKLIST *

Name and Address	No. in Family	No. of Children	Accepted	Refused

* *GUEST CHECKLIST* *

Name and Address	No. in Family	No. of Children	Accepted	Refused

* GUEST CHECKLIST *

Name and Address	No. in Family	No. of Children	Accepted	Refused

* GUEST CHECKLIST *

Name and Address	No. in Family	No. of Children	Accepted	Refused

* GUEST CHECKLIST *

Name and Address	No. in Family	No. of Children	Accepted	Refused

6

Photographs and Videos

Your wedding photographs will be an immediate visual reminder of your big day throughout the years to come, so it is worth making sure you have a good photographer, who will record your wedding day as you want to remember it.

You will almost certainly want to employ a professional photographer, unless you are planning a very small, civil wedding, or have a friend who is particularly skilled at photography. A professional will be used to getting the co-operation of crowds of people in posing for pictures, and knowing exactly what shots are needed. Professional firms are also insured, so if the film was damaged, you would be entitled to compensation. Professionals tend to produce formal wedding pictures but are perfectly capable of taking more candid shots too, if you ask them.

As a backup, it pays to ask one or two friends who have reasonable cameras and usually take good pictures, to shoot a couple of rolls of informal, 'natural' pictures.

Choosing a photographer

Go to a firm which specialises in wedding photography – you will find advertisements in the local press, Yellow Pages or bridal magazines or, better still, ask friends for recommendations. Visit several photographers to compare both the style and standard of their work, and the likely cost. Different firms have different methods of charging. Some charge for each print, others have an extra fee for attending the wedding, while yet others offer a package deal of so many shots for a set price, with extra prints charged on top.

Make it clear if you want the photographer to come to the bride's home before the ceremony, if you want pictures taken of the guests arriving at the church, at the reception, and of the couple leaving. If you have any particular requests, mention these in advance too (see checklist, page 48).

If you want any pictures with special effects (a misty surround, or a picture imposed on to a different background, for instance), find out if the firm offers these, and the cost.

Many ministers do not allow photographs or videos to be taken during the ceremony, so do ask about this. You may have to be content with pictures of the register being signed and the couple leaving the church.

Once you have found a photographer you feel happy with, book him or her early, to ensure they keep that day free. Finally, make sure you confirm everything in writing.

Organising a video

To have your wedding day on film is a luxury only available in recent years. If you can afford it, it gives a unique record of the day and will be especially enjoyed by any guest unable to be there with you. As with photography, you can choose whether you want an amateur or professional job. Only opt for a home recording if you have a friend who is experienced with videos, and whom you know will produce an acceptable film, otherwise the end result could be very disappointing. It is possible to hire the equipment quite cheaply; look in your Yellow Pages for local rental firms.

There are various points for the amateur video-user to remember which will help achieve a good result. The first is to make a plan of which scenes to record and work out in advance, if possible, the best position from which to capture each one. Remember to keep the camera as steady as possible, mounting it on a tripod when necessary. Don't overdo your use of the zoom lens and keep each sequence fairly short – 10-20 seconds is a good average to aim for. You can keep a check on the sound recording by using headphones.

Hiring a professional is more expensive and, as for photographers, you should shop around for the best deal. Try to see a sample wedding video to make sure you are happy with the style of their work. If you see a film you particularly like, ask for the same cameraman and equipment to be used.

✳ *PHOTOGRAPHY CHECKLIST* ✳

Name and address of photographer

Phone no and name of contact

What fee has been agreed?

When do we pay the fee?

When should the photographer arrive:
 at the bride's home
 at the church

What restrictions are there on
 photography at church/register office?

Is the lighting adequate:
 in the church
 at the reception

Do we want the photographer to
 sell photographs at the reception?

Have we ordered any photographs with special effects?

How much will these cost?

Will the photographer also supply a wedding album?

What will the wedding album cost?

Do we want any other prints in presentation folders
 (as gifts for parents, etc)

When will the proofs be ready?

How long will it take to produce
 final prints after we order?

Do we want glossy or matt prints?

All details confirmed in writing (date)

* *VIDEO CHECKLIST* *

Professional videos

Name and address of video company

Phone no and name of contact

What fee has been agreed?

What does this include?

Is the video allowed inside the church?

What time should the video
cameraman arrive at the church?

Is the lighting adequate:
in the church
at the reception

Do we anticipate any problems with sound recording
(eg traffic noise; loud music at reception)?

Can the original be copied, and what will each copy cost?

When will the video be ready?

All details confirmed in writing (date)

Amateur videos

Name and address of video hire company

Phone no and contact

What is the hire cost?

What does this cover?

When does the equipment have to be returned?

Shooting plan discussed with camera operator

Which shots do we particularly want?
Bride with parents at home
Bride on her own at home
Bride and bridesmaids at home
Bridesmaids helping bride with veil
Guests arriving at church
Best man and groom arriving at church
Bridesmaids arriving at church
Bride and her father arriving at church
Bride walking down the aisle
Ceremony (if allowed): Taking vows
　　　　　　　　　　　　Exchanging rings
　　　　　　　　　　　　Congregation looking on
　　　　　　　　　　　　Couple at altar
Signing the register
Leaving the church
Bride and groom together
Couple with bridesmaids and best man
Bridesmaids together
Bride and groom with bridesmaids
Couple with bride's parents
Couple with groom's parents
Couple with both sets of parents
Couple with all members of both families
Complete wedding group
Leaving the church in wedding car
Guests throwing confetti
Arriving at reception
Receiving line
Informal shots during reception
Close up of ring/s on finger
Speeches: Bride's father
　　　　　　Groom
　　　　　　Best man
Cutting the cake
Bride throwing bouquet
Leaving for honeymoon

7

Choosing the Music

Music can add greatly to the mood of celebration and rejoicing at a wedding ceremony, and help to turn the service into a stirring occasion.

Lists of suitable choices are given on page 54 for pieces of music to be played at the bride's entrance, while the register is being signed, and at the departure of the bridal party, as well as suggestions for hymns and psalms that most people in the congregation are likely to know.

How to choose

Raise the question of music the first time you meet the priest or minister at the church. Most churches have a resident organist, and you might like to talk to him or her personally and discuss your choice. Remember that not every church organist is up to professional standard, nor is every church organ a superb instrument, by any means. Go along to a service to get an idea of the limitations you will need to consider, and choose music that is suited to both the instrument and the musician. A simple piece, well played, is far better than something complicated, performed badly. If you know of a good organist, it may be possible to arrange for him or her to play at your wedding rather than the usual organist.

Unless you have plenty of ideas for music, it's a good idea to ask the organist to suggest a selection of pieces to be played during the 15-20 minutes before the bride arrives, while the guests are waiting. You will then need to decide which piece of music to use for the bride's entry – remember that she shouldn't have to rush down the aisle, so choose something with a fairly steady pace. Select the music used as you leave the church to provide a joyful finish to the service. Your local record library should be able to provide records or cassettes of organ and choral music selections to help you make a choice. **Wedding and Home** magazine produce a cassette of popular wedding tunes too.

Two or three hymns, or two hymns and one psalm, are usually sung during the service. The bride and groom can choose their favourites, bearing in mind their suitability for a wedding. The words of these, plus details of the other music and of the ceremony itself, can be provided for guests on individual Orders of Service. Arrange for these to be printed at the same time as the invitations, remembering to order one for each guest plus a few spares. The ushers should distribute these as guests arrive. If you choose not to have printed Orders of Service, make sure that hymn books and prayer books are available.

The church choir, if you use it, will help to swell the sound during the congregational hymn singing and might even add harmonies and descants. They could also sing a psalm or anthem while you are signing the register. If your church doesn't have a resident choir, you could, with the minister's agreement, see if a local choral society would send some of its members along to sing at your wedding. You might be asked to pay a fee or alternatively make a contribution to choir funds.

To make your service more individual, you could consider using other instruments, such as trumpets, guitars, or perhaps a solo singer or group of musicians to perform some of your favourite music while you are signing the register. Consult the minister to see if he has any objections before you go ahead with this idea. If you choose a favourite pop song, check the words of it carefully beforehand to make sure they are appropriate for the occasion. A song may hold special memories for you both, but may not be very suitable for a wedding ceremony.

Another important 'musical' element for your wedding is the church bells. For payment of a fee to the bellringers, these can be rung both before and after the service, by arrangement with the minister, and will provide a gloriously happy background sound to your wedding.

Traditionally, the bridegroom pays the fees for organist, choir and bellringers. The payments can be put in envelopes for the best man to give to them, or to leave with the minister, on the day.

✳ *MUSIC CHECKLIST* ✳

Organist

Booked: date

Fee

Choir

Booked: date

Fee

Bellringers

Booked: date

Fee

Other musicians

Name

Phone no/contact

Date of booking

Fee

Music for bride's entry

Hymns and psalms (in running order):

1.

2.

3.

Music for signing the register:

1.

2.

Music for leaving the church

Musical choices

At the bride's entry

Wagner: Bridal March from Lohengrin (Here Comes the Bride)
Brahms: Theme from the St Anthony Chorale
Wesley: Choral Song
Purcell: Trumpet Tune and Air
Boyce: Trumpet Voluntary
Handel: Minuet from the Royal Fireworks
Handel: Arrival of the Queen of Sheba
Parry: Bridal March

Popular hymns and psalms

Love Divine, All Loves Excelling
Praise My Soul the King of Heaven
O Perfect Love
Come Down, O Love Divine
Lead Us, Heavenly Father, Lead Us
Praise to the Lord, the Almighty
Glorious Things of Thee are Spoken
Guide Me, O Thou Great Redeemer
The King of Love, My Shepherd Is
Immortal, Invisible
Now Thank We All Our God
The Lord's My Shepherd (Psalm 23, to the tune Crimond)
Great is the Lord (Psalm 48)

While the register is signed

Bach: Jesu Joy of Man's Desiring (organ solo, or with choir)
Gounod: Ave Maria (choir or soloist)
God Be In My Head (choir or soloist)
Mozart: Laudate Dominum (choir or soloist)
Mozart: Exultate Jubilate (soloist)

As you leave the church

Widor: Toccata
Mendelssohn: Wedding March from A Midsummer Night's Dream
Pachelbel: Toccata in C
Dubois: Toccata in G

8

How to Get There

Arriving in style is all part of the fun of getting married. The type of transport you choose will depend on how formal you want to be, how far you have to travel and, possibly, the time of year.

For a traditional white wedding, it is customary to hire smart limousines, such as Daimlers, Rovers, or, of course, Rolls Royces. You may be given the choice of a black or white model, and you can ask for the car to be decked out with fluttering ribbons.

If your budget won't run to this, ask around among family or friends who have suitable cars to see if anyone can help out. If the cars are given a good wash and polish and are decorated in style on the day, you can still make an impressive entrance.

Bear in mind that if you are wearing a very full or flounced dress you will need to travel in a fairly large car to avoid crushing the skirt. Daimlers, Dorchesters and Rolls Royces are suitably roomy, although fairly expensive to hire.

Something unusual Some firms can offer vintage cars which are more expensive than modern vehicles. They do get booked up early, however. Some models are open-topped, leaving you at the mercy of the weather! Although it sounds like fun to travel to the church in full view of passers-by, you will find that the wind wreaks havoc with veil and hair, so allow time to take the journey very slowly.

If your journey is reasonably short, and not along too busy a road, or up any extremely steep hills, then a horse and carriage is an idea that may appeal to you, although again you need to be reasonably confident of a dry day. Covered carriages (known as broughams) can also be hired, and these are drawn by a single horse or a pair, depending on the size of the carriage. Again, allow plenty of time for the journey.

Making the arrangements

You will certainly need one car to collect the bride and her father from home and take them to the church. The same car will take the newly-weds to the reception. A second car will probably be needed to transport the bridesmaids. The bride's mother can travel with the bridesmaids if there is room in the car. If not, you should make arrangements for her to be given a lift to the church by friends or family.

Usually the best man drives the groom to church, and can then use his own car to get to the reception. Alternatively, he can travel to the reception with the bridesmaids.

It is also the best man's duty to make sure that a car is available at the end of the reception for the couple to drive away on honeymoon. You can of course retain the wedding car for this, but most couples prefer to hire something less conspicuous or use their own car. For a really exuberant end to a wedding, you could go away by boat, balloon or even helicopter!

Before you make any bookings, check round local hire firms and compare prices and the types of cars available. Be sure to book well in advance, especially for something un-usual.

For a register office wedding the transport arrangements can be similar to a church wedding, or less formal. The main difference is that the bride and groom can travel to the ceremony together if they wish. Hired chauffeur-driven cars or family cars can be used.

Guests are expected to arrange their own transport, both to the ceremony and reception. However, it is thoughtful if the best man can make sure that everyone is looked after, and perhaps arrange for car-owners to help those who do not have their own transport.

Keep the telephone number of a local taxi company handy at the reception, for guests who need transport home.

✳ *TRANSPORT CHECKLIST* ✳

Hiring the cars

Name and address of hire company

Phone no and name of contact

How many cars do we need?

What type of cars shall we hire?

What colour will the cars be?

Will they be decorated?

Do we want something special – a vintage car,
  or horse and carriage?

What time should the first car arrive:
  to collect the bridesmaids?
  at the church?

What time should the second car arrive:
  to collect the bride and her father?
  at the church?

What time will the cars leave the church for the reception?

How much will the car hire cost?

All details confirmed in writing (date)

Other transport arrangements

Have we arranged to borrow any cars we need?

Will the best man take the groom to church?

How will the best man get to the reception?

How will the bride's mother travel from church to reception?

Are we going to hire a car to go on honeymoon?

If not, how shall we get our own car to the reception?

Do any of our guests need transport to the ceremony or reception?
Details of lifts arranged:

9

The Wedding Flowers

Fresh flowers are a key part of any wedding, and it is worth choosing them carefully, and taking expert advice. Used imaginatively, wedding flowers can pull together your colour theme as well as making the wedding surroundings festive.

It's safest to have your bouquet made professionally by a florist unless someone in the family is exceptionally skilled with flowers. Making a bouquet is a time-consuming and tricky task that is best not tackled by an amateur. However, you might be able to save money by asking friends or family to take care of flowers for the church or reception.

Another possibility for the ceremony is to see if the parishioners who usually take care of flowers in the church can prepare special arrangements for you. Have a word with your minister about this.

The bridal bouquet

The bouquet is a focal point in itself but should also complement your wedding dress. Choose the flowers carefully to suit your outfit. An elaborate dress might call for a lavish bouquet, while a romantic 'country look' dress would be set off beautifully by a loosely wired sheaf of garden flowers. And to complement a very simple outfit you might choose to carry a single beautiful bloom – perhaps a lily or a rose.

The bridesmaids' flowers can be smaller, simpler versions of the bride's bouquet or may use blooms with stronger colours. Little girls could carry tiny posies, flower-filled baskets, or balls of flowers, attached to their wrists by ribbon loops. Don't give children anything too big or difficult to hold. You can vary the bridesmaids' flowers if you wish, choosing one style for children and something bigger or more sophisticated for the adults.

Choosing the shape Several different shapes are commonly used for bouquets. When deciding, bear in mind your height and build, as well as the style of your dress. Long, narrow bouquets are more flattering to brides with broad hips!

Round bouquets can be large and packed with generous-sized flowers; or can take the form of a smaller, neater posy. Ribbons or foliage can trail down decoratively from the bouquet. Teardrop or cascade bouquets are roughly triangular in shape; fronds of leaves or trailing flowers are often used to soften the outline. Sheaves or sprays of flowers look very natural and can be simply tied with ribbon, but they may be awkward to hold easily.

What colour?   A pure white or cream bouquet with touches of green foliage can look very effective. Discuss the choice of white flowers with your florist and take a swatch of fabric along if possible – if your dress is a very brilliant blue-white, white flowers could look yellow by contrast, so be careful.

Mixtures of creamy flowers and pastels – peach or apricot, pink or pale yellow – look very fresh and delicate. Or you could go for a stronger colour, such as russet, gold or deep pink, either alone or mixed with flowers in paler tones of the same colour. Take into account your own colouring and that of your bridesmaids when choosing. You will obviously want the flowers to tone with the bridesmaids' dresses, or you might like to pick out a shade from their sashes or from a trim on your own dress, and echo it in the flowers.

Which flowers?   Your choice will be influenced by the season, the style of the wedding and your budget. You will save money by choosing flowers that are in season, cutting down on the number of different flowers you use, and opting for a simple arrangement.

Be imaginative in your choice. You may have one or two favourite flowers that you want to include, and a colour theme to work to, but ask your florist for advice and look at pictures in magazines as well as florists' portfolios, for inspiration. Country flowers such as marigolds, cornflowers or daisies can look just as effective in the right setting as more formal roses and carnations. Always try to add some foliage –

ivy or ferns are both good.

Lilies and orchids are beautifully formal, perfect choices with a very elegant dress. Delicate spring blossoms such as primroses and violets would be charming for a petite bride, or you could express a flamboyant nature with a brilliantly colourful bouquet of crimson peonies or richly scented ivory gardenias.

An unusual idea for an autumn or winter wedding would be to use dried flowers and leaves. These are available in many stunning colours, both deep and pastel, and the bouquets can be kept afterwards. Silk flowers are another popular everlasting alternative.

After the ceremony, if you don't follow tradition and toss your flowers into the crowd as you leave the reception, you might like to have your bouquet preserved. Several firms do this, so make enquiries beforehand and arrange for the bouquet to be stored somewhere cool and taken for pressing as soon as possible.

The language of flowers   Traditionally, certain flowers have special meanings, so you could compose a bouquet which contains a secret message!

Carnation – pure, deep love
Cornflower – hope
Forget-me-not – true love
Gypsophila – fertility
Ivy – fidelity, the marriage bond
Lily of the valley – renewed happiness
Orange blossom – a lucky marriage
Rose (red) – I love you; *(white)* – I am worthy of you
Violet – fidelity

Headdresses

There are lots of different ways to use fresh flowers in headdresses, both for bride and bridesmaids. One large blossom or a spray can be simply tucked into the hair; or you can do something more contrived and wire the flowers into halos, circlets, garlands, wreaths, flower-decked Alice bands, combs or slides. Trails of tiny flowers and greenery can be skilfully entwined in your hair if your hairdresser can do this. For most headdresses delicate flowers look best.

Link the choice of flowers with those you are carrying and choose varieties that won't wilt: roses, freesias, lilies, lilies of the valley, cornflowers and carnations are all long-lasting.

Buttonholes

It is usual for the male members of the wedding party to wear a buttonhole and you can also provide them for all the other guests if you wish. Carnations are the most popular choice, or you could have roses or lilies of the valley instead. Choose white, or pick a colour to go with your scheme.

It's a thoughtful gesture to provide corsages for the bride's and groom's mothers. These can be made up by the florist – check to see what colours would be most appropriate to go with the outfits being worn.

Flowers for the church

Once you've established with the minister that there is no objection to the flowers you have in mind, and worked out who will be arranging them, you can choose exactly what floral arrangements to have in the church.

Pew ends are tied on the end of each row of pews, so that they line the aisle. They can be in the shape of rings or hearts, or small posies. You could also attach similar arrangements to iron balustrades and choir stalls, hang them below wall lights, or place them high up on window sills.

One or two larger arrangements on the altar steps can look magnificent. Choose colours that blend with your overall theme. Pale or bright shades work best in church, as they help bring a blaze of light to dark corners. Go for striking rather than intricate designs. The flowers will be seen from a distance, and subtle details will be lost.

For the register office Many register offices are already decorated with flower arrangements – ask in advance if you want to supply your own. You, and your bridesmaid(s) if you have them, can carry flowers but these are best kept fairly simple.

Flowers for the reception

If your reception is being held at a hotel or restaurant you may find that floral decorations are provided as part of the package. The arrangements will be made by the proprietors, although you should be able to request a particular design or colour scheme, provided there is no other reception on the same day.

Flowers help to continue the celebratory feeling throughout the reception. You can have arrangements of varying sizes standing on side tables and window sills. Try to arrange for a larger, eye-catching display to be placed so that it is seen as the guests enter.

For a formal sit-down meal you can have small arrangements placed at intervals along the tables, with perhaps slightly larger or more ornate displays for the top table. Or you might like to have a small spray or posy at each guest's place setting, to be taken home.

For a buffet meal, small arrrangements can be placed on the table where the food is laid out, and also at the tables if you are providing seating. You could also edge the main table with swags of fresh flowers and leaves.

The cake may be topped with a few fresh or silk flowers if you wish, or can be surrounded by a garland of flowers. Again, the table on which it stands can be decorated with loops of trailing flowers and foliage. Choose flowers to match those used in the bride's bouquet which is often displayed on this table during the reception.

If you are having the reception at home, buy or pick enough flowers to fill the house with fragrance. Garlands can be hung on doors, ropes of flowers draped across mantelpieces or twisted around banisters. You could even make an archway of flowers leading out into the garden. Enlist the help of friends to decorate the house early on the wedding morning.

For home-made flower arrangements, you will need to do some forward planning. Order the flowers that are not coming from your own garden in good time (be generous). Arrangements in vases can be done the day before the wedding, and left to stand somewhere cool overnight. If you are making garlands, do these last of all and put them outside, covered, overnight in a shallow container of water to keep fresh. Pin them in position on the day and spray other arrangements with water as you put them in position.

You might like to order a couple of bouquets and hide them away to present to your mothers as a surprise gift and thank-you just as you are leaving for your honeymoon.

* FLOWERS CHECKLIST *

Name and address of florist

Phone no and name of contact

Details of bride's bouquet

Bridesmaids' flowers: details and number ordered

No and type of buttonholes

No and type of corsages

Details of flowers for the church

Who will arrange flowers in the church?
Name, phone no

Details of flowers for reception

Who will arrange the flowers for the reception?
Name, phone no

All details confirmed in writing (date)

10

Wedding Presents

As soon as you have announced that you are getting married, people will start asking you what you would like for a wedding present. In order to avoid duplication, and also to make sure of receiving gifts they would choose for themselves, most couples make up a wedding present list.

Of course, it is entirely up to your guests to decide whether to buy something from the list, or to use their own initiative and buy you a present of their own choosing. This may be something more individual and non-practical such as a picture or a case of wine. These gifts can give the couple much pleasure, but most guests will probably prefer to play safe and choose an item from the list.

The bride and groom can enjoy shopping around together and choosing the items they would like to have as presents. The wedding list is a golden opportunity to equip your home with all you need, and this will very much depend on whether one of you, or both of you, already have a place of your own. If you have a fairly well-stocked home already, take this chance to be treated to some more special pieces of glassware, china, bed linen and so on.

The list should specify make, style, design name or number, colour or pattern and number of each item required. Include things that span a wide price range. If you are asking for any very expensive gifts, such as a food processor, several people can club together to buy it for you. A complete dinner service can be broken down so that different people can buy pieces from it.

Distributing the list   There are several ways to distribute the gift list. Perhaps the best method is to make a master list, photocopy it, and send copies to guests who ask to see it. You can ask them either to cross off the item they are buying and return their copy to you, or simply to phone or drop you a line so that you can keep the master list up to date.

You could also circulate a single list and ask guests to send it on, but this takes longer and is a less reliable way of making sure that everyone who wants to see the list gets a look at it in time. Don't send the list to guests unless they specifically ask for it, however.

Another possibility is to place your list at one or more specific shops. Your choice will be restricted to the stock carried by the chosen shop but a large department store will have most domestic things. The bride's service at the store will arrange for gifts to be sent to you as they are purchased, and will keep you informed of what has been bought and by whom. Guests visit the shop to inspect the list, which is kept constantly up-to-date, and make their selection.

The wedding gift list

Putting together a gift list can be great fun. The lists on pages 65-68 will help act as a checklist and possible source of inspiration, but what you include will depend on what you have already, and on your own lifestyle. The designs and colours specified will of course reflect your taste.

If you enjoy cooking and plan to do lots of entertaining, you will need a good collection of pots, pans and equipment, plus enough crockery and glasses for dinner parties. Will you be using a freezer and/or microwave? Make sure you ask for suitable dishes. Does your new home have a garden? Spades and forks can go on the list, as well as outdoor leisure items, such as barbecues, garden chairs and lighting. Towels and bed linen will be chosen to go with your colour schemes, and you could even ask for ready-made curtains, roller blinds and rugs if you are furnishing a home from scratch. Start planning your list well in advance of the wedding, as it takes lots of time and thought to get it right.

The Kitchen
Baking tins
Bread bin
Breadboard/knife

Broom
Can opener
Casseroles: large,
    small, flameproof

Cheese grater
Chopping board
Colander
Coffee grinder
Coffee maker
Deep fryer
Dishwasher
Double saucepan
Draining rack
Dust pan and brush
Electric carving knife
Electric kettle
Flan dishes
Food processor
Frying pan
Grapefruit knife
Iron
Ironing board
Kitchen bin
Kitchen scissors
Kitchen tool set
Knives
Knife sharpener
Liquidiser
Measuring jug
Microwave oven
Mixing bowls
Oven gloves
Pressure cooker
Ramekins
Refrigerator
Rolling pin
Salad dryer
Saucepans
Scales
Slow cooker
Soufflé dishes
Spice rack

Storage jars
Tea towels
Timer
Toasted sandwich maker
Toaster
Trays
Vegetable rack
Washing up bowl
Whisk
Wok
Wooden spoons
Yoghurt maker

Bedroom and bathroom
Alarm clock
Bath mat
Bathroom cabinet
Bathroom scales
Bedside lamps
Bedspread
Blankets
Clock radio
Duvet
Duvet covers
Electric blanket
Linen basket
Mirror
Pillow cases
Pillows
Rugs
Sheets
Towels:
    Bath
    Guest
    Hand
Valance

Living room
Clock

Coffee table
Cushions
Lamps
Mirror
Photograph frames
Radio
Rugs
Stereo
Television
Trolley
Vases
Video
Wastepaper bin

Dining room

Glass
Aperitif glasses
Beer glasses
Brandy glasses
Carafe
Champagne glasses
Cocktail shaker
Decanter
Fruit bowl
Liqueur glasses
Sherry glasses
Tumblers
Water jug and glasses
Wine glasses
Whisky glasses

China
Cereal bowls
Coffee cups and saucers
Coffee pot
Cream jug
Dinner service:
    Dessert plates
    Dinner plates

Fruit bowls
Meat plate
Sauce boat
Serving dishes
Side plates
Soup bowls
Egg cups
Gravy boat
Milk jug and sugar bowl
Mugs
Serving dishes
Soup tureen
Tea cups and saucers
Teapot
Vegetable dishes

Cutlery
Canteen of cutlery
Carving set
Coffee spoons
Fish knives and forks
Ladle
Pastry forks
Salad servers
Serving spoons
Steak knives and forks
Teaspoons

Miscellaneous household
Butter dish
Candlesticks
Cheeseboard and knife
Coasters
Condiment set
Corkscrew
Curtains and blinds
Diy tools
Heated plate or trolley
Ice bucket

Napkin rings

Napkins

Nut crackers

Place mats

Salad bowl

Salt and pepper mills

Sweet dishes

Tablecloths

Toast rack

Tumble dryer

Vacuum cleaner

Washing machine

Wine cooler

Wine rack

The Garden

Barbecue

Fork

Garden seating

Lawnmower

Secateurs

Shrubs and plants

Spade

Trowel

Saying thank-you

It can be a real problem to keep track of the gifts once they start to arrive in large numbers. You should keep an up-to-date list (use the one on pages 69-72), of exactly what has been given. Send thank-you notes as you receive the gifts. For presents brought on the day, make sure labels are kept with gifts to identify them. Send letters when you return from honeymoon.

Everyone should be thanked in writing, and if you use printed 'thank-you' cards, do write on a personal note to each giver, so that they feel their gift is really appreciated. Most people go to a lot of trouble to choose a present that will be liked, and are very pleased to receive a personal thank-you, even if it arrives some time after the big event.

Thank-you letter for a wedding present

Thank you very much for the casserole you sent us as a wedding present. It's the perfect size for two and you couldn't have picked a better colour than that lovely cheerful red, which looks great in our new grey and white kitchen. We've given it pride of place on one of our dresser shelves, so it's on full view.

We have been back from honeymoon for a week now, and the wedding seems like a lifetime ago because there's been so much to do in the house. It's all a bit chaotic at the moment, but once we're sorted out you must come over and see our handiwork. Until then, thanks again from both of us for such a thoughtful present, which will give us pleasure both to use and to look at for years to come.

* WEDDING PRESENT CHECKLIST *

Gift	Given by	Thank-you sent (date)

* WEDDING PRESENT CHECKLIST *

Gift	Given by	Thank-you sent (date)

* WEDDING PRESENT CHECKLIST *

Gift	Given by	Thank-you sent (date)

* WEDDING PRESENT CHECKLIST *

Gift	Given by	Thank-you sent (date)

11

Planning the Reception

As soon as you have set the date, place and time of your wedding, you can start organising the reception. First of all you will need to decide what sort of reception appeals to you. A full-scale sit-down meal, followed by music and dancing in the evening, is the most expensive option. A buffet meal cuts down on the cost of hiring serving staff; or for a reception which ends in the late afternoon, you could simply serve a choice of hot or cold canapés. Some couples decide to have a small reception for family and close friends only and invite friends to an informal party later on. Others keep the numbers down for the meal and invite a second contingent of guests to come along and join the reception in the evening.

Whatever you decide, remember that popular venues get booked up well in advance, so plan ahead in order not to be disappointed.

Where to hold the reception

The choice of venue depends very much on the number of guests and how formal you want to be. If you opt for a large hotel or restaurant, the catering arrangements can be easily taken care of and all the organisational details can be left to the management.

A less expensive possibility is to hire a church hall or perhaps a room in a local civic centre. These can be very attractive – or rather shabby – so do check before you book. Make sure there are suitable facilities for preparing food and clearing up.

Holding the reception at the bride's home requires a lot of work on the part of her family, but can make for a very relaxed and informal atmosphere. Take careful account of the size of the house when drawing up the guest list – no one enjoys being crammed in like a sardine, so make sure you do

---

✳ *RECEPTION VENUE CHECKLIST* ✳

Name and address of venue

Phone no and name of contact

What time can the wedding party arrive at the venue?

Can someone visit the venue earlier on the day to check the arrangements?

What time do we have to leave the venue?

Are the catering arrangements included?

Does the venue have a licence to serve alcohol?

Will the bar staff need to apply for an extension to their licence?

Is there adequate parking nearby?

Are the cloakroom/toilet facilities suitable?

Is there adequate seating?

Are there enough tables?

How many serving staff will be on duty?

Is there somewhere secure where wedding presents can be kept?

Is there a room where the bride and groom can change?

Arrangements made in writing (date)

Arrangements confirmed in writing (date)

---

have enough room to accommodate everyone comfortably.

If you have a large garden, and are planning a summer wedding, consider hiring a marquee. This can be a traditional canvas tent, or a modern, free-standing frame tent. With these, the walls can be rolled up if the weather is hot, so that guests can look out into the garden. You will need to discuss with the hire company suitable flooring, and details of how and when the tent will be erected.

For something really unusual, you might like to hold a floating reception, on board a boat. Or perhaps a local stately home has rooms or gardens available for receptions.

Bear in mind the distance of the reception venue from the church – ideally it should be no more than a few minutes' drive. If the route is complicated, it's thoughtful to provide a map, which you can sketch yourself, so that your guests can find the way easily.

If you feel daunted by the idea of organising a reception, there are companies (who often advertise in bridal magazines) who will take the job over for you.

Important details

Make sure that some seating is available, even if you are not having a sit-down meal. Receptions can be tiring, and people may be glad of a chance to rest their feet! If you are having a buffet, decide whether you want tables and chairs provided for the meal, or if guests are going to eat standing up. If so, bear this in mind when choosing the food.

Young children easily get bored, and it's wise to provide a room where they can play, out of harm's way, if this is possible.

Make sure that there is a room where the couple's luggage can be kept until they leave, and where they can change into their going-away clothes.

Check the cloakroom facilities, making sure that they are clean and adequate. For a winter wedding you will need a place where coats can safely be left.

Think about the little touches that will make all the difference to your reception. Do you want flowers on the tables? Would you like specially printed napkins, place cards or tablecloths – if so, these need to be ordered in plenty of time. If you want to go to town on extras like this, printed balloons, place mats, books of matches and crackers are all possibilities. You can even organise a massive banner printed with the couple's names; or lay on a celebratory firework display.

Is there somewhere for the wedding gifts to be kept safely, and does the venue have suitable insurance?

Work out the timing carefully. Don't leave guests hanging around too long before food is served, and make sure you allow enough time for speeches, cake-cutting and so on before you have to get changed ready to leave for the honeymoon.

Music

If you are planning a reception that goes on into the evening, you will want to provide some music or entertainment. Check your local Yellow Pages or newspapers for details of discos, bands, pianists and other types of musical entertainment. If possible, make a booking on the strength of a personal recommendation. Decide what sort of music you want, remembering the mix of age groups to be catered for, and check that this choice can be offered by the band or DJ you have chosen.

When you book, discuss exactly how long you want the music to play for; how many breaks there will be and for how long; what time the music is to begin. Make a point of asking for the volume to be kept to a level where people can still make themselves heard. Traditionally, bride and groom take the floor first and when they have danced for a few minutes alone, other guests can join them. The couple may like to request a special or significant song for their first dance together, and this should obviously be discussed before the day.

Food

The type of food you choose for your reception will depend on whether the reception is large or small, formal or informal. Is it taking place in the afternoon or evening? How tight is your budget? For a large, formal reception, where money is no object, you might opt for a three- or four-course sit-down meal. If the reception continues into the evening you could also provide light snacks later on such as sandwiches or cake and tea or coffee.

At a more informal reception, where guests are likely to be

eating standing up, you could have a help-yourself buffet, or employ staff to bring round a selection of hot and cold finger foods, which people can nibble as they chat and still have a hand free to hold their glass.

If the reception is being held at a hotel, then the catering arrangements will be part of the overall 'package'. However, if you are using a hall or other venue, you will have to decide whether to use a firm of caterers, or prepare the food yourself. Bear in mind the problems of transporting the food to the reception if you do this, and arrange for clearing up afterwards.

Choosing the menu It's worth comparing menus and quotes from a number of caterers before reaching a decision.

Check whether any of your guests have special requirements, such as vegetarian or kosher diets, especially if you are planning a sit-down meal where no choice of food will be offered. Otherwise dishes such as roast meats are generally safest for this type of meal, as you can be fairly sure of pleasing everyone. With a buffet or finger food you can afford to be a bit more adventurous and offer a selection which includes some more exciting foods.

Doing your own catering If you decide to do the cooking yourself, make sure you get organised well in advance, and enlist as much help as you can. Make detailed lists of everything that needs to be done and work out who is going to be asked to do what.

You will need extra freezer space, so try to arrange this with neighbours and friends very early on. You could even consider hiring an extra fridge and freezer. Although the bride and her mother might do much of the advance preparation themselves, they will both be fully occupied looking after the guests on the day, so friends and relatives will need to be asked to take responsibility for much of the work at the reception itself: setting the food out, serving and clearing away. Alternatively, you could hire waitresses through a caterer or employment agency, or use reliable teenagers or students.

Planning the food A finger buffet sounds like an easy option, but in fact it takes a lot of time and organisation to prepare a sizeable selection of nibbles. Choose food that can be eaten in one bite and that won't drip or crumble. Be fairly generous with fillings however, as you don't want to leave guests with a mouthful of dry bread or pastry. Hot nibbles are delicious, but make sure that you can serve them at the right temperature: not so hot that your guests' mouths and fingers are burned, not so cool that the canapés have become greasy.

For inspiration you can scan cookery books and magazines. Don't choose anything over-elaborate, highly spiced or fiddly to prepare. Give any new recipes a trial run before making a definite decision.

Hot canapés Baby quiches, tartlets and pizzas with varied fillings and toppings; nuggets of chicken or fish, marinaded in herby dressing; sticks of satay with peanut sauce dip; tiny meat balls with an accompanying dip; giant prawns; stuffed pastry parcels; stuffed vine leaves.

Cold canapés Little sandwiches; stuffed mushrooms; asparagus or smoked salmon wrapped in thin brown bread; crab claws or vegetable sticks with a dip; tiny pieces of toast topped with pâté.

At a finger buffet, offer eight or nine different canapés and allow 12 or more bites per person.

Another option is to serve a cold buffet lunch. You could start by offering a small selection of canapés, say half-a-dozen different types, with an allowance of five or six bites per person. Follow these with a main course such as cold salmon, cold roast joints or turkey, or a selection of quiches. Serve several salads, one or two based mainly on salad vegetables; another based on rice or pasta, one on potato or beans. The possibilities are endless.

For dessert you can offer fresh fruit – strawberries or raspberries – and cream. If you feel more ambitious, slices of gâteaux, trifle, syllabub or chocolate mousse will all go down well.

Laying out the buffet Well ahead of the day, count up how much equipment you can accumulate in the way of crockery, cutlery and glasses. Remember that you will need serving plates and cutlery, flower vases and ashtrays as well. You will also need the means to make large quantities of tea or coffee, plus cups, saucers, milk jugs and sugar bowls. Borrow or hire anything that you are lacking.

Organise the buffet table so that guests start at one end and work down to the other; or start from either end and finish in the middle, without overlapping. They should be able to pick up a plate, cutlery and napkin first. It will be easier and quicker for people to serve themselves if the food is presented on several smaller platters, rather than one or two huge ones. Cut food into portions before you lay it out: this saves both time and wastage. Keep some dishes and garnishes in reserve, so that the table can be replenished when necessary. Allow plenty of serving spoons.

Countdown to preparing your own wedding meal

Four or more weeks ahead

✻ Start making and freezing all the food which can be frozen.
✻ Make a list as you go along of all the garnishes that will be needed.
✻ Decide exactly what you need to hire or borrow and make the necessary arrangements.

One week ahead

✻ Double-check that you have enough crockery, cutlery, glasses, cloths etc and arrange to hire any extras that may be needed.
✻ Confirm orders for drink, hired goods, staff.
✻ Make any dressings and garnishes (such as croutons) that can be kept refrigerated until needed.
✻ Later in the week make dishes that can be kept for a couple of days in the refrigerator.

Two days ahead

* Shop for cheese and biscuits; fruit; garnishes.

The day before

* Do as much preparation as possible.
* Prepare salads late in the day as far as possible. Do not add dressings.
* Remove frozen dishes from the freezer to defrost.
* Lay the buffet table with cloth and cutlery. Put glasses out.

On the day

* Arrange for someone to set the food out and add decorations and garnishes no more than two hours before the reception is due to start.
* Place hot savouries on baking trays ready for reheating.
* Place the wines to chill.
* At the last possible minute, dress the salads and take desserts out of the refrigerator.

The wedding cake

Your cake will be the focal point of the reception, and you will want it to be very special. The number of tiers will depend on how many guests are invited. Remember to include those who cannot be present, but who would appreciate being sent a slice of cake later on.

Think about what shape the cake should be, whether you would like any special decoration, or whether the icing should be of a particular shade to tie in with your colour scheme. Although most brides have a fruit cake with white icing, you could equally choose to have a sponge cake or chocolate cake.

You can buy decorations for the top of the cake from stationers, or you may prefer to have a small fresh flower arrangement: if so, remember to include this in your florist's order.

The cake can be made by a professional baker and should be ordered around two months in advance. You may, of course, have a friend or relative who can do it, or might prefer to make the cake yourself.

Making your own cake

A rich fruit cake, arranged in tiers and lavishly iced and decorated, is the traditional cake for weddings. You will find that mixing a rich fruit cake is quite hard work and that the baking time is long. If it is more convenient you can mix the ingredients one day and bake the cake the next: when the mixture is ready, put it in the cake tin, cover loosely with a clean cloth and leave it in a cool place (not the fridge) until you are ready to bake it.

What size cake?   When making a tiered cake it is essential to get the proportions of the tiers correct, to give the desired pyramid effect. Don't attempt to make the bigger sizes of cake unless you have a really large oven, as you should allow at least 2.5cm (1 inch) space between the oven walls and the tin. For a three-tiered cake, bake the two smaller cakes together and the largest separately.

Three-tiered cakes   To serve around 130 people, use a 30.5cm (12 inch) cake; a 20.5cm (8 inch) cake and a 15cm (6 inch) cake.

To serve around 100 people, use a 28cm (11 inch) cake; an 18cm (7 inch) cake and a 12.5cm (5 inch) cake.

The smallest base you should use for a three-tiered cake is 28cm (11 inch).

Two-tiered cakes   To serve around 110 people, use a 30.5cm (12 inch) cake and an 18cm (7 inch) cake.

To serve around 60 people, use a 25.5cm (10 inch) cake with a 15cm (6 inch) cake.

The smallest base you should use for a two-tiered cake is 25.5cm (10 inch).

Preparing the tins   Stand the tin on a double thickness of greaseproof paper, draw round the base and cut out two shapes. Cut a strip of greaseproof long enough to go round

Rich Fruit Cake

Note: when baking large cakes 20 cm (10 inch) and upwards, it is advisable to reduce the oven heat to 130°C (250°F) mark ½ after two-thirds of the cooking time.

Square tin (side)	12.5 cm (5 in)	15 cm (6 in)	18 cm (7 in)	20.5 cm (8 in)
Round tin (diameter)	15 cm (6 in)	18 cm (7 in)	20.5 cm (8 in)	23 cm (9 in)
Approximate liquid capacity of mixture	600 ml (1 pint)	1 litre (1¾ pints)	1.4 litres (2½ pints)	1.8 litres (3¼ pints)
Portions	16	20	28	36
Approx cooked weight	900 kg (2 lb)	1.1 kg (2½ lb)	1.6 kg (3½ lb)	2.2 kg (4½ lb)
Ingredients				
Currants	200 g (7 oz)	225 g (8 oz)	350 g (12 oz)	400 g (14 oz)
Sultanas	75 g (3 oz)	100 g (4 oz)	125 g (4½ oz)	175 g (6 oz)
Seedless raisins	75 g (3 oz)	100 g (4 oz)	125 g (4½ oz)	175 g (6 oz)
Glacé cherries	50 g (2 oz)	50 g (2 oz)	75 g (3 oz)	125 g (4½ oz)
Mixed peel	25 g (1 oz)	25 g (1 oz)	50 g (2 oz)	75 g (3 oz)
Flaked almonds	25 g (1 oz)	25 g (1 oz)	50 g (2 oz)	50 g (2 oz)
Lemon rind (as a fraction of a lemon)	a little	a little	a little	a little
Plain flour	150 g (5 oz)	175 g (6 oz)	200 g (7 oz)	300 g (11 oz)
Mixed spice	1.25 ml (¼ level tsp)	1.25 ml (¼ level tsp)	2.5 ml (½ level tsp)	2.5 ml (½ level tsp)
Cinnamon	1.25 ml (¼ level tsp)	1.25 ml (½ level tsp)	2.5 ml (½ level tsp)	2.5 ml (½ level tsp)
Butter	125 g (4½ oz)	150 g (5 oz)	175 g (6 oz)	250 g (9 oz)
Dark brown soft sugar	125 g (4½ oz)	150 g (5 oz)	175 g (6 oz)	250 g (9 oz)
Eggs, beaten	2	2½	3	4
Brandy	15 ml (1 tbsp)	15 ml (1 tbsp)	15 ml (1 tbsp)	15–30 ml (1–2 tbsp)
Approx cooking time	2½ hrs	2½–3 hrs	3 hrs	3½ hrs

82

3cm (9in)	25.5cm (10in)	28cm (11in)	30.5cm (12in)	33cm (13in)
5.5cm (10in)	28cm (11in)	30.5cm (12in)	33cm (13in)	35.5cm (14in)
.7litres (½pints)	4.1litres (7¼pints)	4.5litres (8pints)	6litres (10½pints)	6.6litres (11½pints)
8	72	92	120	136
.7kg (6lb)	4kg (9lb)	5.2kg (11½lb)	6.7kg (15lb)	7.7kg (17lb)
25g (1lb 6oz)	775g (1lb 12oz)	1.1kg (2lb 8oz)	1.5kg (3lb 4oz)	1.7kg (3lb 12oz)
25g (8oz)	375g (13oz)	400g (14oz)	525g (1lb 3oz)	625g (1lb 6oz)
25g (8oz)	375g (13oz)	400g (14oz)	525g (1lb 3oz)	625g (1lb 6oz)
75g (6oz)	250g (9oz)	275g (10oz)	350g (12oz)	425g (15oz)
00g (4oz)	150g (5oz)	200g (7oz)	250g (9oz)	275g (10oz)
00g (4oz)	150g (5oz)	200g (7oz)	250g (9oz)	275g (10oz)
lemon	¼ lemon	½ lemon	½ lemon	1 lemon
00g (14oz)	600g (1lb 5oz)	700g (1lb 8oz)	825g (1lb 13oz)	1kg (2lb 6oz)
ml (level tsp)	5ml (1level tsp)	10ml (2level tsp)	12.5ml (2½level tsp)	12.5ml (2½level tsp)
ml (level tsp)	5ml (2level tsp)	10ml (2level tsp)	12.5ml (2½level tsp)	12.5ml (2½level tsp)
50g (12oz)	500g (1lb 2oz)	600g (1lb 5oz)	800g (1lb 12oz)	950g (2lb 2oz)
50g (12oz)	500g (1lb 2oz)	600g (1lb 5oz)	800g (1lb 12oz)	950g (2lb 2oz)
	9	11	14	17
0ml (2tbsp)	30–45ml (2–3tbsp)	45ml (3tbsp)	60ml (4tbsp)	90ml (6tbsp)
hrs	5½hrs	7hrs	8hrs	8½hrs

the edge of the tin, with an overlap, and just over twice the height of the tin. Fold this strip in half lengthways, then make a 1cm (½ inch) fold along one long edge and snip up to the crease at 1cm (½ inch) spaces.

Grease the base of the tin with melted margarine and place one of the base pieces of paper inside. Grease this paper and the sides of the tin, then place the long strip of paper round the inside with the snipped edge at the base. Press on to the sides of the tin, smoothing well, brush the folded edge with more margarine and place the second base piece on top.

Protect the outside of the cake from overbrowning by wrapping a double thickness of brown paper around the outside of the tin.

Ingredients   The chart on pages 82-83 indicates the quantities of ingredients required to make rich fruit cakes in the standard range of square and round tins. If you are using an irregular shaped tin, you can calculate the amount of mixture needed by filling a tin with water, measuring the water, and checking the chart to find the cake with same or nearest liquid capacity.

The mixture has to be slightly stiffer than usual to support the weight of the fruit: if it is too wet the fruit could sink to the bottom. Remember that all dried fruit should be thoroughly cleaned and dried before use and glacé cherries should be rinsed to remove any excess syrup, then dried. Toss all fruit in a little of the measured flour before using.

Method

1. Pick over dried fruit to remove any stalks, etc.
2. Halve or quarter glacé cherries, chop the flaked almonds.
3. Sift together the flour and spices. Add the grated lemon rind.
4. Cream the butter and gradually beat in the sugar. (A large food mixer is ideal for this job. Divide the mixture in half and cream in two batches if making very large quantities.)
5. Beat in the eggs a little at a time. If the mixture shows signs of curdling, beat in 15-30ml (1-2 tbsp) of the measured flour.
6. Fold in the remaining flour followed by the fruit, nuts and brandy. (When making very large quantities it is easier to use

a clean washing-up bowl and mix with the hands.)

7. Spoon the mixture into the prepared tin(s). Level the surface using the back of a spoon. Hollow out the centre of the cake slightly so that the top will be level when cooked.

8. Stand the tin on several thicknesses of brown paper or newspaper, on a baking sheet, in the oven, and cover the top of the cake towards the end of cooking if necessary. Bake in the oven on the lowest shelf at 150°C (300°F) mark 2 for the time stated on the chart. Check the cake half-way through cooking. If it seems to be browning too quickly, reduce the heat to 130°C (250°F) mark ½. Do this automatically when baking large cakes.

9. If you know that your oven is hot, then cook for less than the stated time; if it is slow, cook for longer. For fan ovens adjust the cooking times and temperatures in line with the manufacturer's instructions. Test the cakes before removing from the oven by inserting a fine, warmed skewer into the centre. It should come out clean when the cake is done.

10. Allow the cake to cool in the tin.

11. When cold, wrap the cake in greaseproof paper and then in foil, making sure that it is completely covered. Store in a cool, dry place until ready to ice the cake. This cake is best left for about 3 months to mature before using. If liked, unwrap every 2-3 weeks, prick the surface with a fine skewer, and spoon over a little brandy or other spirit.

Finishing the cake Almond paste or marzipan creates a smooth foundation for the icing and protects the cake from discolouring the decoration. Ready-made almond paste is a better choice than home-made, as it is less likely to discolour the icing. When buying, be sure to choose the white variety, not the yellow. Check that it is fresh, as old stock may have hardened at the edges. Quantities are given in the chart on pages 82-83.

Icing a wedding cake is a skilled job which is best left to the experts unless you are very confident. Look in your Yellow Pages for professional cake-decorators, or enquire at a local bakers.

Storing a tier Some people like to keep the top tier of their wedding cake to use as a christening cake for their first child. If you want to do this, wrap the cake, plus any other leftovers, tightly in greaseproof paper and then in kitchen foil. If any cake is kept for longer than two months, the marzipan and icing should be removed and the cake re-iced shortly before it is needed.

Drink

If you are hiring a reception venue, it could pay you to do some comparison of wine prices before you make firm arrangements. Sometimes it is cheaper to buy your own drink (most wine shops do this on a sale-or-return basis), but your caterers may charge corkage. If you decide to provide your own drink, make sure the caterers are providing ice, glasses and any other bar equipment.

What to serve Although it is an appealing idea to serve Champagne, or good sparkling wine, right through the reception, this can become very costly. For a reception lasting three hours, most guests will consume half a bottle of wine, and for a longer reception the tally could reach a bottle a head. Naturally some guests will drink much less than this, and offering non-alcoholic alternatives can help to save on the amount of alcohol needed. But it is always best to over-estimate, rather than run out.

It is a false economy to serve cheap sparkling wine, as it is likely to leave your guests with massive hangovers. A better option is to serve a still white wine at first – perhaps a medium dry, light wine from Germany or Alsace – and bring out the Champagne for the toasts. If you are on a very tight budget, the toasts could be drunk in a sparkling white or rosé wine instead, or with the same white wine which was served during the meal.

Sparkling wines and champagne can be 'stretched' by mixing with orange juice (Buck's Fizz). You can turn ordinary white sparkling wine a pretty shade of pink by adding a dessertspoon of crème de cassis (a blackcurrant liqueur) to each bottle and mixing gently.

You can offer sherry as an alternative to wine at the start of the reception, in which case give guests the choice of medium (amontillado) or dry (fino).

You may need to choose a drier white wine, such as a Chablis or Graves, to go with the wedding meal, and also a light red such as Chianti Classico or Côtes du Rhone. Non-alcoholic drinks – mineral water and good fruit juices – should be available throughout the reception.

Arrange for tea or coffee to be served when the meal has ended.

DIY drink If you are doing your own organising at home, shop around at local off-licences to get the best sale-or-return and glass-hire deal that you can find. Most off-licences will hire glasses to you free provided you buy your wine from them and at some you can even return the glasses unwashed, which saves an enormous chore. Hire enough glasses for at least one-and-a-half times the number of guests invited.

Off-licences may also be able to sell you ice in bulk, or you might be able to buy ice delivered to your door (check in your local telephone directory). A bag weighing 12.6kg (28lb) is only about the same size as a large cushion and will last for ages unless the weather is exceptionally hot. To keep your white wine cool, put it in plastic rubbish bins, lined with plastic sacks and filled with ice and water. It takes about an hour for one case of wine to chill; chilled bottles should be moved to the top of the bin as more bottles are added. You can open still white wine in advance, and replace the corks gently in the necks of the bottles.

✳ FOOD AND DRINK CHECKLIST ✳

Caterers

Name and address of caterers

Phone no and name of contact

Which menu have we chosen?

Cost per head

Does this include VAT?

What drinks have we chosen: on arrival
with the meal
for the toasts
other

Cost of drinks

How many waiters/waitresses do we need?

Will the bar be open?

What amount of money are we putting behind the bar?

All arrangements made in writing (date)

Confirmed in writing (date)

Preparing the food yourself

Who can offer fridge/freezer space?

Who will help with: the cooking
serving
setting out
clearing up

Where will non-frozen food be stored?

Where will food be kept before serving on the day?

Where can we hire cutlery and crockery?
Name, address and phone no

Name, address and phone no of drink suppliers

Drink ordered (date). Will they deliver?

Glass hire/ice supplies arranged

Wedding etiquette

Even if your wedding is very informal, there are certain conventions and traditions without which no reception would be complete.

Arrivals The convention here is a receiving line, which gives all the guests a chance to congratulate the newly-weds, and also to thank their host and hostess – normally the bride's parents. For this reason it is important that the bride's parents arrive at the reception ahead of everyone else. The groom's parents should also be in the receiving line and, if you wish, the best man and attendants can also greet the guests. At a very informal wedding, the guests can be greeted by the bride and groom on their own.

The receiving line should wait until all the guests have arrived before starting the meal. For a sit-down reception, the bridal party proceed to the top table (see seating plan below), and the guests then find their places. Name cards can be put at each place, or for a large gathering, display a seating plan where people can easily see it. Give some careful thought to who sits where. Put couples near each other and seat people attending the wedding on their own near someone who can be relied on to make them feel welcome. Try to make sure that the guests don't break down into camps by mingling friends and family of bride and groom together.

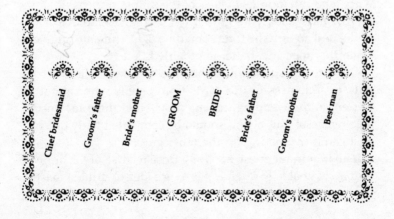

Chief bridesmaid · Groom's father · Bride's mother · GROOM · BRIDE · Bride's father · Groom's mother · Best man

Toasts and speeches

These follow after the meal, and the golden rule is – keep them short! The idea is to wish the couple well, and to thank the appropriate people.

First of all, the bride's father makes a speech. If he is not present, then the speech will be made by whoever gave the bride away, perhaps another relative or an old friend of the family. This speech is likely to be fairly serious. The father should say how happy he is with his daughter's choice of husband, perhaps give one or two anecdotes from her childhood, and end with a toast to the bride and groom. The guests are asked to raise their glasses and drink to the couple.

Next it's the turn of the groom to reply on behalf of his new wife and himself. The purpose of his speech is to make sure that everyone who has taken part in organising the wedding is properly thanked.

The bride's parents should be thanked for the wedding, and the guests for their gifts. Make sure no one is left out – if friends or relatives helped in the catering, made the cake or the dresses, this is the time to see to it that their efforts are publicly acknowledged. Finally, the bridegroom thanks the attendants for doing such a marvellous job, and proposes a toast to the bridesmaids.

Last, but by no means least, the best man rises to his feet to make the final speech. He has the most opportunity to be witty, and can indulge in tales of the couple's courtship, little known facts about the groom (with commiserations to the bride) and so on. The tone should be light and amusing, and again this speech is better kept fairly brief.

Once he has spoken, it is then the best man's duty to read out any Telemessages or cards from people who cannot be present at the wedding, having first vetted them for unsuitable remarks! This again, should be completed fairly quickly, as it can prove boring for the other guests.

If an important guest, such as a close relative of the bride or groom, is unable to attend, it is a nice idea to drink a toast to absent friends at this point.

Cutting the cake The best man continues his duties by announcing the cutting of the cake. The bride holds the knife and the groom lays his hand over hers as together they make the first cut. It may be easier to have the cut started beforehand, so that the couple don't have to struggle with hard icing! In some regions it is traditional to cut the cake before the meal. One token cut is all that is needed before the cake is removed, divided into small slices and distributed to the guests as quickly as possible.

The remains of the cake should be kept aside, so that slices can be sent out to absent relatives and friends. Special cake boxes can be bought from stationers for sending the cake. Alternatively, you could order special boxes printed with your initials.

Leaving the reception

Once the formalities are finished, the dancing, if any, can begin. And finally, the bride and groom get changed ready to leave. The bridesmaids should help the bride to dress.

Make arrangements for someone to take care of your wedding clothes. The bride's mother will look after the wedding dress, and the groom's clothes may need to be returned to the hirer, or taken for cleaning.

Once the couple are ready to leave, the best man should announce their departure. There is then a round of farewells, the bride tosses her bouquet into the crowd (unless she decides to keep it to be pressed or preserved); and the pair depart in a flurry of confetti.

It's a wise idea to keep the honeymoon car hidden before departing. It is all too easy for enthusiastic guests to overdo their 'sabotage' and get the couple off to an unhappy start, in a car drenched in shaving foam or smothered in impossible-to-remove lipstick. The couple may prefer to leave the reception by taxi or hired car; especially if they are concerned about the amount of alcohol they may have consumed during the festivities. Another possibility is to enlist the help of a friend who is a non-drinker to drive the couple away.

12

What to Wear

Your perfect wedding dress might be a cloud of white satin, a simple design in cotton lawn, or a bold and colourful outfit to wear to the register office. The choice is as wide as you care to make it.

Buy, hire, or make?

Consider your budget – can you afford to splash out on a one-off designer dress, or must you lower your sights? If you want something totally glamorous and can't afford to buy, then hiring might be the answer. Big hire firms should be able to offer a reasonable selection, and if you see one you like, you will need to book the dress well in advance.

If you are a talented dressmaker or there is one in the family, then you might still be able to have something unique, which won't break the bank. Scour pictures in bridal magazines and the pattern books in a large store – you may come across the exact style you want, and if not, you'll certainly get plenty of inspiration. A good needlewoman should be able to adapt a pattern as you want it, or even design a dress from scratch. If the dress is being sewn at home, it's an excellent idea to make it up first in a cheap fabric, to check that the fit and style are just right before the fabric for the actual wedding dress is cut out.

If these skills are beyond you, you could go to a professional dressmaker. Her services won't be cheap, but you should end up with a dress that fits perfectly and has been made to your precise specification.

If you decide to buy, you'll have plenty of choice. There are several chains selling only bridal outfits and many large stores have well-stocked wedding-dress departments too. When buying, pick a day when you have plenty of time. Take someone whose judgement you trust (this won't necessarily be your mother!) and try on plenty of different styles. Take a good look at both front and back views and don't make any hurried decisions. This is the dress of a lifetime, and deserves to be chosen carefully.

A stunning style

Styles of wedding dress are not at the mercy of current fashion, and the only important thing is to choose a style that suits you – your personality, your proportions and your colouring. It is particularly important to get the scale right for a church wedding, and to emphasize height. Many wedding dress styles borrow freely from periods of history: medieval gowns, Victorian or Edwardian styles of dress to the more recent Twenties or Thirties styles.

Your height and figure are determining factors. Are you petite, with small bones and a slender waist? You could look swamped in a full-skirted, ruffled dress. Which suits you best – a high neck, or something with a gentler line, cut a little lower? Try both to see which flatters your face and neck. Are you a typical pear-shape, with small bust and wider hips? A figure-skimming line, that doesn't fit too closely at the waist, will look good. Are you big-busted? A boned bodice, or draped design, can help put your figure into proportion.

The time of year will have some bearing on length of sleeves and fabric; in the winter months you may have to wrap up in a heavier brocade or velvet.

Remember that the back view of your dress is very important, as that is all the congregation will see during the service. Look for extra details, such as a bow or a sash, to add interest. Dresses with trains are very formal, and flow down the aisle beautifully. But beware if you plan to dance the night away at your reception – it may be possible to detach the train, but if not you might decide instead to get changed early on in the evening. Of course, there's no reason why your wedding dress has to be full-length. Ankle-skimming, mid-calf or shorter – dresses are available in every length.

What about colour? Most brides still opt for the traditional white, but even this can look very different according to the fabric you choose. Smooth satin has a deep sheen, cotton looks crisp and fresh, velvet is rich and sumptuous. You could choose a fabric that is embroidered or embossed with a pattern, also in white.

White doesn't suit everyone and there are various other options. Ivory, silver or any shade of cream could look equally attractive. Pastel shades of palest pink, apricot or lemon can be very subtle. Daring brides could choose a brighter colour – or even black! The choice is yours – be as traditional or outrageous as you like, but whatever you choose, make sure you can carry it off. Remember all eyes will be on you!

Veils and headdresses

An elegant wedding gown calls for a very special headdress, and nothing sets the dress off more effectively than a cloud of veiling. Choose the length carefully, to complement the style of the dress. Shoulder length is attractive and manageable, or for a grand wedding in a large church you could have a 'cathedral length' veil to waft behind you down to the ground. Some veils are designed to be piled high on the head, while others stream out from a comb or Alice band. Whatever style you choose, make sure the veil is firmly anchored to your hair, and cannot easily be moved by someone accidentally treading on it or by a strong gust of wind.

A veil can be completely plain and unadorned, or can have a scalloped or patterned edge. It could have a straight or ruffled lace or ribbon border, or be edged with a glittering trim. Or a shower of lace flowers, stars or other motifs could be stitched on to it.

Lace, either antique or new, makes a marvellously rich-looking veil. You may even be lucky enough to have one in the family. If you are using an old veil, take it with you when you choose your dress. Lace gradually yellows with age, and you will have to select a dress that tones with it. White would probably be too much of a contrast.

Your veil can be attached to a headdress, or you may prefer to dispense with a veil and just wear a headdress on its own. Whatever you decide, the choice is wide, and there are dozens of styles on offer: a circlet or band of flowers, fresh or silk; a head-hugging Juliet cap, perhaps decorated with beadwork or embroidery; a tiara; a single bloom or cluster of flowers; a flurry of ribbons. You can be as understated or as flamboyant as you wish.

Some dresses are offset better by a hat than a headdress. A summery, ballet-length dress would look pretty with a broad brimmed picture hat or a straw hat, trimmed with fresh flowers. An Edwardian frock that has a bustle and short train looks superb with a large hat, decked with feathers or big silk roses.

Try lots of different styles before making up your mind and remember that how you wear your hair will influence the final effect.

Accessories

Your most important accessory could be the one no one sees – your underwear! Buy a well-fitting bra before you shop or are fitted for the dress. Choose a plain style – lace and other trimmings might show through – and opt for flesh pink, peach or cream, which will be less visible than white if your dress is at all see-through. Wear the bra at home for a few hours before the day to make sure that it doesn't cut in or ride up.

If you are having a body-hugging, svelte style dress, make sure you wear pants that have an ultra-smooth fit, with no bulge. French knickers or silky camisoles are lovely, but best saved for the honeymoon as they can be uncomfortable if worn all day.

If you need a big, full petticoat or two to give your skirt width and volume, look in bridal shops, or check bridal magazines for mail order advertisements. Some bridal shops will hire hooped petticoats, which will save you the expense of buying one.

Decide between stockings – cool and glamorous – or tights – warmer and more comfortable – and buy a couple of pairs in case of emergencies. Many shops stock tights and stockings embellished with hearts or bows.

Shoes, although they will hardly be seen, are important. Very high heels are out – you don't want to teeter down the aisle, or get caught up when you try to stand after the prayers. But shoes with a low heel may be more comfortable than a completely flat pair. Remember, you'll be on your feet for a lot of the time, both during the wedding and at the reception. Make sure the soles are non-slip and wear the shoes round the house for a few hours before the day to 'break them in' and make sure they are comfortable. If you can't find the exact colour you want in the shops, buy plain white satin pumps and have them dyed. The bridal shop may arrange this for you. Alternatively, dye them yourself or ask at a shoemending shop.

Other accessories, such as white parasols and lace gloves, are available at bridal shops and can add a very pretty touch. Parasols are usually for decoration only and have no practical use. Make sure that your chauffeur has a white umbrella if there is any possibility of rain on the day, so that you can get to and from the car in the dry.

When it comes to jewellery, simple items are best. A scoop-neck or low-cut dress could leave your neck looking a bit bare without a necklace, so choose a simple gold chain, or a string or two of pearls. Earrings should be fairly small, and pearl studs or drops, or a gold design would be appropriate. You can wear a fine bracelet and pretty watch if your wrists are on show, but you may prefer not to wear any rings other than your engagement and wedding rings.

Remember, when planning your outfit, that many brides like to observe the old custom of 'Something old, something new, something borrowed, something blue'. A blue or ribboned garter worn just above the knee is a traditional item you might like to have for a bit of fun, perhaps to show in a photo or two.

Dressing for the register office

You can wear whatever you like to be married in a register office. Some brides like to marry in a traditional wedding dress, complete with veil and bouquet, especially if they are marrying for the first time. If you want to do this, choose a style that is fairly simple, without a train. The groom and other men can wear morning dress, or might feel slightly less formal in lounge suits. Don't forget to order a buttonhole for the groom – perhaps choosing a colour to match your dress.

Alternatively, you could wear a dress with a festive and bridal look to it, in white or a pale colour, such as pink, lemon or peach. A simple headdress could be worn with an outfit like this, and you could also carry a posy of flowers or a small bouquet. You may like to provide a small posy for your female witness to hold.

Other brides break away from tradition completely and choose an extra-special suit or dress that can be worn again. Find a style that isn't too tailored and add a corsage of flowers, or some beautiful jewellery. Finish the outfit with an elegant bag (not too big) and shoes (avoid very high heels), and perhaps a stylish hat. If you do choose a hat, opt for a fairly small, neat style which will not hide your face in the photographs.

Going-away outfits

This is your second chance of the day to make a big impression. You'll only be seen fleetingly in your going-away clothes, but it's still worth taking time and trouble when choosing them, especially as many guests will be taking photographs as you leave.

A suit or dress with a jacket or coat to wear on top if the weather dictates would both be appropriate. Many brides seize the chance to sport a hat – make sure it can be easily worn with your wedding day hairstyle.

Of course, everything depends on where you are heading for – if your next stop is the airport and a long flight, you'll want something that's easy and comfortable to wear, as well as looking pretty. Bear in mind the climate at your destination – there is nothing worse than landing in a hot country dressed in thick clothes. But if you're being whisked away to a smart hotel for a romantic dinner together, then a more dressy outfit would be ideal. Remember that you will need tights, shoes and a bag as well.

Don't forget your groom's going-away outfit. If he wore a lounge suit for the ceremony, there's no need for him to change unless he wants to be more casually dressed for a long journey. But if he wears morning dress he could change into a smart suit, which he may already own, or into something more relaxed. Be sure to discuss this well in advance, so that you can agree on the type of clothes you want before you go off on shopping expeditions.

Clothes for the bridesmaids and page boys

The first decision is whether the clothes will be bought, hired or made specially, by you, a friend or relative, or a professional dressmaker. If you are having several bridesmaids, it will certainly save money if their dresses are made by a friend or relative rather than bought.

You can choose from a range of dresses to buy or hire at any of the bridal specialists. Hiring is a sensible option if the dresses you want are suitable only to be worn on the one occasion.

Traditionally, the bride's parents pay for the bridemaids' dresses, but often these days the attendants (or their parents, if they are children) offer to pay for their own clothes, especially if you have chosen a design that they can wear in the future.

Start early if the dresses are being made, so that they are all ready in time. Allow for late adjustments to fit, especially for children who are still growing.

Which style to choose? Aim for an overall harmony in the theme of the wedding. You don't have to stick rigidly to one style or fabric.

∗ *Do you want the dresses to be in a similar style to your own?* They could follow the same line, but be less elaborate, perhaps with fewer, or simpler decorative touches. If the dresses are being made, you may well find that there is a pattern for bridesmaids specially designed to complement your wedding dress. But do be considerate, especially towards adult bridesmaids. If they are a totally different build from you, the effect of dressing them in a similar style could be disastrous! Be flexible, and choose a design that will be as flattering as possible to each individual.

∗ *What age are the bridesmaids?* A style which looks charming on a three-year-old, could look ridiculous on a 23-year-old. But it doesn't mean that all bridesmaids have to be the same age. Vary the styles to suit the wearers – the adults could wear elegant dresses, while the children have frillier frocks – and you can bring the whole thing together by using toning fabrics.

Bear in mind that young bridesmaids will inevitably let off steam at the reception, and be prepared for the dresses to come in for some rough and tumble. Little girls look sweet in floor-length dresses, but are less likely to trip in mid-calf or knee-length.

∗ *Choose colours to suit the bridesmaids' colouring* If you have a mix of blondes and brunettes, fair and dark complexions, it could be impossible to pick a single shade that suits all. A clever way round this is to use tones of one colour – such as a delicate pale pink twinned with a darker rose. Or some bridesmaids could wear dresses made of plain fabric and others could wear prints. Be adventurous in your choice of materials – pastels are very attractive, but bright tones can be dramatic. Patterns can be bold and splashy, or tiny and discreet. Another idea is to dress the bridesmaids in white, and give them coloured sashes and accessories.

Some brides have one child as a flower girl, and she can be dressed differently from the bridesmaids, perhaps in a floral-patterned dress.

Accessories Headdresses should be simple and in a style that echoes your own. Circlets of flowers, or single blooms, firmly pinned in place, would be suitable. Try to avoid headdresses that involve putting the hair up for younger children, unless they can be relied on to keep every hair in place, all day! Loose hair can be curled or ringletted for the occasion.

Shoes should be comfortable and non-slip. Plain pumps or ballet shoes look good on bridesmaids of any age, and can be dyed to any colour you choose. Older attendants might prefer a style that has a low heel (but make sure they won't tower over you). Shiny black patent could also fit in with some colour schemes. Choose pretty tights or socks to complete the outfits.

Page boys

The little boys in the family needn't feel left out, and might even enjoy dressing up as page boys. Traditional outfits include miniature sailor's uniforms; a Highland look, complete with kilt and sporran; or velvet pantaloons and waistcoat, with a full-sleeved shirt underneath. If the page boys are a bit older they could wear the same type of clothes as the groom and best man.

Clothes for the groom and best man

Choosing suitable outfits for the men is easy – there really isn't a great deal of choice! The bride's father, groom's father and ushers should wear the same style of clothing as the groom and best man. Other male guests are not obliged to wear morning dress, even if the groom is doing so, although they may if they wish. If they decide not to, a smart lounge suit is an appropriate alternative.

Morning dress If you are having a big white wedding and the bride will be in a traditional dress, then the groom usually wears morning clothes.

Traditionally this includes a black tail coat, dark striped trousers, a grey waistcoat, wing-collared white shirt with a silver-grey cravat and a grey top hat – and very smart it looks too.

Grey morning dress is also popular and looks slightly less formal. It may be worn with an ordinary collar and a grey tie. Make sure everyone knows which type you have chosen, so that all the men wear the same.

Morning suits are extremely expensive to buy and are unlikely to be worn very often. For this reason, most grooms hire their wedding outfit. Choose a reputable firm and visit them in advance for a fitting so that you can reserve the right size. Find out how far in advance the suit can be picked up, when it has to be returned (the best man can do this for you, assuming that he hires a suit from the same outlet), and whether it should be dry cleaned before returning.

You will be able to hire all the accessories at the same time. The outfit may come with a pair of grey gloves – tradition demands that these are carried, and not worn. The outfit can be completed with a discreet tie-pin, neat cufflinks and perhaps even a fob watch.

Finally, make sure you have a suitable pair of black shoes that are comfortable enough to be worn all day, and a pair of dark socks – these are the details that tend to be overlooked until the very last moment!

If other male guests are reluctant to climb into the full regalia of topper and tails, but still want to wear something that fits in with the rest of the party, they may be able to hire lounge suits in a similar style to morning dress, with dark jacket and striped trousers.

Lounge suits For less formal church weddings, or register offices, a lounge suit is ideal. You have the choice to buy – off-the-peg, or made-to-measure – or hire. You may already own a suitable outfit.

Colour and style are entirely up to the individual. Dark grey or navy blue look smart, brown more informal. For a summer wedding you could go for a pale suit in beige or even white. The best man should choose his clothes carefully – there is no need for his suit to be identical in colour or style, but it should certainly echo the mood set by the groom's choice, whether it be formal or relaxed.

There's no need to stick to a white shirt if you don't want to, and a colourful or patterned tie would add dash to a dark suit. Consult your bride before you make your choice, to see what colour scheme she is using for her bridesmaids and the flowers, then pick a tie that tones in. Check on the colour of your buttonhole to avoid a clash.

Shoes and socks should be picked specially to go with the colour of your suit. And again, you might like to finish the outfit off with a tie-pin, cufflinks and watch.

The bride's mother

The bride's mother has a very important role on the day, and she will certainly want to choose a new outfit in which she feels and looks her best.

Search for something smart and stylish which is also comfortable. Your mother may also want her outfit to tone in with the general colour scheme – without detracting from the star of the show, of course! You may like to check what the groom's mother is planning to wear to avoid the two mothers having similar outfits, or choosing colours which clash with each other.

A suit (but not too tailored or severe) with an attractive blouse underneath, or a dress and matching jacket in a fine wool or silk would be ideal. For a summer wedding a printed or plain dress would be fine (but equip yourself with a suitable cover-up just in case the day turns chilly).

Matching accessories – shoes, bag and gloves – will help to bring the outfit together. And most women will welcome the opportunity to treat themselves to a glamorous hat, and possibly a change of hairstyle to go with it. Remember that large-brimmed hats, although very eye-catching, tend to overshadow the face in photographs.

* WEDDING CLOTHES CHECKLIST *

The bride's dress

Contact and phone no

Ordered (date)

Date of fitting/s

When can the dress be collected?

Headdress

Shoes

Accessories

Underwear bought

Going-away outfit bought

The bridesmaids' dresses

Ordered (date)

Fitting/s

When can the dresses be collected?

Bridesmaids' headdresses

Bridesmaids' shoes

Bridesmaids' accessories

The groom's clothes

Morning suit booked for hire

When can the suit be collected?

When must the suit be returned?

Has the groom bought a going-away outfit?

13

Bridal Beauty

Forward planning and a trial run for hair and make-up are the keys to looking your radiant best on the day. If you start doing the groundwork on your appearance as soon as you set the date, this will pay stunning dividends by the time the wedding day comes round.

Advance planning

First of all, consider your weight. If you are happy as you are, fine, but if not, and you would prefer to be a little more slender as you walk down the aisle, now's the time to act.

There's no need for drastic diets, but a switch to healthier eating, with plenty of fresh fruit and vegetables, and a ban on sweets and cakes, will soon start to show where it matters. Many brides find that they lose weight naturally with all the rushing around that has to be done before the wedding, combined with nerves, so don't overdo your weight loss regime – after all, it's important that you keep fit and well. Try taking some extra exercise, such as swimming or cycling, to get flabby muscles in trim and put you into good shape if you are bound for the beach on honeymoon. If you are really desperate to shed a few pounds – or want a break from the preparations – you could book a few days at a health farm, a month or so before the wedding. It's a surefire way to whittle off an inch or two, but be warned, it could make a sizeable hole in your budget.

Skin care also needs to be planned, as it takes a while for the effects of a new beauty routine to start to show. A good diet will help keep skin and hair in top condition. Treat yourself to some good quality skin care products and use them regularly. A thorough cleansing, toning and moisturising routine will keep your face looking good. Act now to tackle obstinate spots or blackheads (a beautician will be able to advise you) or any visible facial hair that bothers you.

Treat rough skin on upper arms, thighs, elbows and feet with a loofah or massage mitt every day in your bath, and then apply plenty of body lotion. You'll soon start to see an improvement.

Hand care

Your hands and nails will be the focus of attention on the day, when you show off your wedding ring and cut the cake. If your nails tend to be weak, keep them fairly short, be sure to eat sensibly, and apply nutritious nail creams regularly. If you usually wear polish, give your nails a rest for a couple of weeks before the wedding, to make sure they are good and strong on the day, with no last-minute breaks.

The day before the wedding, relax and give yourself a manicure. Shape nails carefully with an emery board, push back the cuticles gently, and apply a good hand cream. Finally buff your nails to a gentle shine, or apply nail polish. Pale, cloudy colours are more suitable than bright reds or crimsons, especially if you are wearing white. If you prefer, you can paint your nails on the morning of the wedding, when there will be less likelihood of chipping, but make sure you leave plenty of time for the polish to dry thoroughly.

Beauty treatments

Many brides make their wedding an excuse to lash out on beauty treatments such as facials, mud baths or sunbed sessions – and why not? Do be sure though to have your treatments well before the wedding. Facials and heat treatments tend to draw out impurities and can cause a crop of spots to appear a day or two later.

A light tan will look good against white and give you a healthy glow for the photographs. Have your last sunbed session at least a week before the wedding to avoid any skin reactions.

Unwanted hair can be bleached or removed by electrolysis. If you prefer waxing, allow a couple of days for any redness

to disappear. The same goes for professional eyebrow plucking.

Choosing your make-up

Even if you don't usually use much make-up, you will need
to wear a fair bit on the day. White can have the effect of
draining colour, and you want your face to stand out clearly
in photographs and videos, as well as looking good in both
daylight and artificial light.

If you have an uneven skin tone, you can improve matters
with a light foundation that is as close as possible to your
natural colour. Choose a good brand, that won't clog, and
apply it lightly. Buy an emergency cover-up stick in the same
tone, to deal with the odd spot. A dusting of translucent
powder will keep your complexion matt and will provide a
good base for the rest of your make-up.

Blusher will give your face colour, but don't be too heavy
handed. You're likely to be flushed with excitement, nerves
and champagne anyway, so a touch of pinkish or tawny
blusher is all that you should need.

Eyes need emphasising, but avoid brilliant blues and
greens, and opt instead for subtler browns and grey. Be
careful with highlighter – it can stand out unnaturally in
photographs. And go easy on eyeliner and mascara, choosing
neutral shades that aren't harsh, and applying with a light
hand.

Don't forget your lipstick – pale pinks or corals are pretty,
but you might need a brighter shade to counteract the white
dress and balance the rest of your make-up. Steer clear of
anything too dark, however, which could look 'jammy' in
photographs. For a lipstick with real staying power, opt for
one of the long-lasting brands.

Try out all your make-up before the day itself, preferably
while wearing your dress. Study the effect carefully, in
different lights, and make sure you are absolutely happy with
the results. If you are trying a new look, or are wearing more
cosmetics than usual, have a couple of run-throughs until

✻ BEAUTY CHECKLIST ✻

Do I want any beauty treatments? Date booked...

Sunbed sessions

Facial

Sauna

Eyelash dyeing

Eyebrow plucking

Leg wax

Bikini-line wax

Hair bleaching or electrolysis

Manicure

Pedicure

Beautician: make-up lesson

Wedding weight goal

Hairdresser: trial run booked
            wedding day appointment

---

you feel completely confident that you can apply your make-up easily and expertly.

On the day, cover your face with a scarf as you slip your dress over your head, and don't apply lipstick until you have the dress on. A light spray with your favourite eau de toilette (but not one that's too heavy or spicy) completes the picture.

Ask your chief bridesmaid or your mother to carry a make-up kit for you so that you can retouch your face at the church, if necessary, or at the reception.

Hair care

Condition your hair meticulously and keep the ends trimmed regularly in the months leading up to the wedding. If you are planning a major hair treatment, such as a perm or colour, have it done in good time.

Once you have chosen your headdress or hat, take it along to your hairdresser to discuss a suitable style. Long hair tends to look more flattering if it is brushed back off the face or put up, as long as the style isn't too severe. Shorter styles can be prettied up with curls or colour. You may need to use extra spray or mousse on the day to ensure that your hair stays in place immaculately all day. Remember that the style you choose should be manageable enough to adapt easily when it's time to get changed for going away.

On the day, apply your make-up before you go to the hairdresser, so that you don't have to scrape your newly-done hair back from your face later on. You can always retouch the make-up later on.

14

The Honeymoon

Most couples feel in need of a holiday after all the pressure and excitement leading up to the wedding, culminating in the big day itself. Organising – and participating in – a wedding is very tiring, so even if you can only manage a few days by yourselves, do try to get away somewhere peaceful.

When to leave

Some couples leave the reception and disappear in search of sunshine the same evening. This is fine if you can get yourselves organised, with all your packing done beforehand, and travel arrangements made to fit in with the timing of your wedding. But sometimes it just isn't possible to dovetail events, and you may have a day or two in between the wedding and the start of your honeymoon proper. Or your reception may go on into the evening, making it impossible for you to travel far afield on the same day.

It's not a bad idea to arrange to go on holiday the day following the wedding, and spend your first night at a comfortable hotel. This will give you a chance to wind down and recover from the day's events, without having to embark on a long journey straight away.

Many hotels offer special facilities for honeymoon couples, including four-poster beds, bottles of Champagne, flowers and so on, if you feel like treating yourselves.

Whatever you decide, you will need to make some arrangements in advance. You will both need to have your going-away clothes and luggage brought to the reception. Make sure you have the tickets, passports, if needed, and other documents, and that someone will look after them until you are ready to leave.

Decide how you are going to get from the reception to your wedding night destination. If you are driving your own car, be prepared for guests to have 'decorated' it for you. The only way to avoid this is to hide the car beforehand – not always very easy!

Where to go

The choice of destination will depend on how much time and money you have to spare. It will also be very much influenced by the kind of holidays you both like. Not everyone enjoys lounging on a beach for two weeks – you might prefer to go walking, cycling, or birdwatching.

When making your choice, bear in mind that you will want time to relax, and a touring holiday that involves a lot of travel, or an activity holiday that sounds fairly strenuous, may not be appropriate.

Some couples like to make this the holiday of a lifetime, and splurge on a fortnight soaking up the sun somewhere very exotic. This is a particularly good idea if you are marrying in winter, when the chances of finding good weather close to home are remote.

If you are going somewhere unusual, find out in good time whether you will need a visa – some countries are very slow to issue these. If any injections are required, have them well before the wedding, and time them for days when your programme is not too busy. Check your passports well in advance. If the bride wishes to change her name, she needs to apply in good time (forms are available from main post offices). Although it's a very romantic idea for the groom to organise a surprise honeymoon, in practice it makes life rather difficult for the bride, who cannot plan her wardrobe until she knows where she is going.

Island holidays are traditional for honeymoons, but pick your paradise with care. Some of the less expensive Greek destinations, for example, can become uncomfortably over-crowded, especially in high season, and are best avoided if you are searching for uninterrupted togetherness.

Perhaps the ultimate in hedonistic honeymooning is to splash out on a luxury cruise in warm waters, where there will be nothing to do all day but laze in the sun between occasional bursts of sightseeing. City holidays can be very exciting, whether you choose a romantic European destination such as Venice or Paris or head off to New York or even further. Aim for a few days of total relaxation as well, though, in order to come back feeling refreshed.

One way to get the best of two worlds is to book a two-centre holiday, with one week spent soaking up sights and culture in a city and the other in the countryside or on the coast.

Of course, there's no need to go abroad on honeymoon. Many people enjoy a break in a part of this country that is new to them, especially if this means staying in unaccustomed luxury in a country hotel. Others like to take the opportunity to move into their new home together and spend a few days settling in.

Honeymooners on a tight budget might be able to 'borrow' a friend's house or cottage for a few nights. And, of course, there's no rule that says you have to spend your honeymoon alone. Some people have a day or two *à deux* before heading off for a houseparty or skiing holiday with friends.

✳ HONEYMOON CHECKLIST ✳

What time must we leave the reception?

Have we booked our first night destination?

How are we getting to our first night destination?

Where will we leave our car during the reception?

Who will take our luggage and going-away clothes to the reception?

Who will look after our travel documents during the wedding?

Have we booked and confirmed our holiday?

Are our passports up to date?

Do we need visas?

Do we need injections?

Have we arranged foreign currency or traveller's cheques?

Who Pays for What

People are much more flexible these days over who foots the different bills. Often couples split some of the costs between themselves, and offer financial help to the bride's family. The following lists will give you a starting point for sorting out the money side of your wedding.

The bride's family pay for:

* Press announcements
* Invitation, service sheets and any other stationery
* The bride's dress and accessories
* The bridesmaids' outfits (but often the bridesmaids, or their parents, if they are small, will pay)
* Flowers for church and reception
* Photographs/video
* Cars to church and reception
* Reception, including hire of venue and all catering
* The cake

The bridegroom pays for:

* Engagement ring
* Wedding ring (but the bride pays for the groom's ring if he has one)
* Licence or registrar's fee, if appropriate
* Church expenses: minister's fee, organist, choir, bell-ringers, tip for the verger, marriage lines
* Flowers for the bride and bridesmaids
* Buttonholes and corsages
* Presents for the bridesmaids, best man and attendants
* Stag night
* Honeymoon

Who Does What

An at-a-glance summary of the roles of each of the main characters involved in the wedding. For more detail, see the previous chapters.

The best man

* Arranges the stag night party
* Organises the ushers
* Gets the groom to the church on time
* Takes care of the ring/s and produces them at the right moment
* Witnesses the signing of the register
* Escorts the chief bridesmaid out of the church
* Pays church fees on the day on the groom's behalf
* Makes a speech at the reception
* May act as master of ceremonies at the reception, announcing toasts, cake-cutting etc

The chief bridesmaid

* Helps the bride to dress
* Keeps an eye on any younger attendants
* Arranges the bride's dress before she enters the church
* Holds the bride's bouquet during the ceremony
* Witnesses the signing of the register

The bride's father

* Travels to church with his daughter
* Escorts her down the aisle
* Gives her away at the appropriate moment in the ceremony
* Witnesses the signing of the register
* Escorts the groom's mother out of the church
* Makes a speech at the reception

The ushers

* Direct guests to their seats in church
* Distribute buttonholes, hymn books or orders of service
* Show the bride's mother to her seat in church

Wedding Day Warnings

Every couple wants the big day to go off as smoothly as possible. Forewarned is forearmed, so here is a list of potential trouble spots which, if you plan ahead for them, needn't cause you any headaches.

At the church

* Cancellation and rescheduling are costly and occasionally necessary due to ill health or family problems. It is possible to insure against this and other disasters – accidental damage to your dress; photographs not coming out.

* Decide early on whether children and babies are welcome at the ceremony and/or reception and plan accordingly. They can disrupt the ceremony disastrously by crying or screaming at the wrong moment. If possible, arrange for tinies to be looked after elsewhere and offer them some amusement at the reception.

* Double check that your *Gone with the Wind* crinoline will fit into that vintage car or horse-drawn trap.

* Don't bring the minister's wrath down on your head by allowing guests to throw confetti if the church frowns on it.

At the reception

* With a large number of guests, the receiving line can stretch for what seems like miles. The least you can do is to offer guests a drink while they wait.

* The best speeches are brief. Remind speech-makers of this fact when they are drafting their witty words.

* Make absolutely sure that whoever drives the couple away from the reception, whether or not it is the groom, stays sober. Don't take any chances on this.

* Keep your car out of sight, to prevent any damage being done to paintwork, when guests 'decorate' your car.

Preparing for Marriage

Your wedding day, important and exciting though it is, is only the beginning. After it comes the rest of your life together, as a couple. Married life is very different from being single, and it often takes a while to adjust, both to the practicalities of living under the same roof, and to the emotional changes which inevitably take place. Even couples who have lived together prior to marriage may find subtle differences after the wedding, as they start to plan for the certainty of a long-term future together.

The right choice

Adjusting to married life is something you can only do with practice. But there is a lot of groundwork you can put in *before* the wedding, by thinking carefully about your future life and discussing it with your partner.

First and foremost – and preferably before you get engaged – do some serious thinking about marriage. What do you and your prospective partner want from marriage, and can you live up to each other's hopes? It's easy for people's judgement to become clouded when they are in love, but being 'in love' is a temporary, if delightful, state. For your marriage to be a success, and for a deep and lasting love to emerge once the headiness of new romance has worn off, you will need a firm foundation of mutual liking and respect. So, spend some time thinking about your partner's special qualities and what they mean to you.

* Do you agree about important issues – and if you disagree, can you do so amicably, with respect for each other's opinions and without coming to blows?

* Are you able to compromise in order to reach a decision that pleases both? If one partner always gets his or her own way, the other can end up feeling resentful.

∗ Does your partner ever behave in a way which you find totally unacceptable, and if so, could you honestly learn to live with this?

∗ What are your partner's feelings about money, children, religion? All or any of these could have an important bearing on your future.

∗ Do you get on with each other's friends and if not, would this cause problems?

∗ Do you and your partner respect and support each other's views?

∗ Do you have some shared interests?

∗ Are you both happy for the other to pursue interests which are not shared?

∗ Can you talk to your partner about anything – including sex – easily and freely?

∗ Is your partner a good friend, someone who can make you laugh, who knows your strengths and weaknesses and accepts them?

∗ What annoys you about your partner, and do you feel able to cope with these irritants, large and small, long term? People seldom change their basic nature, so if your partner's untidiness or spendthrift ways drive you to distraction, think carefully before you take the plunge.

It is not cynical or pessimistic to assess your 'rightness' for each other in this way. After all, marriage is a lifelong commitment and one which, if made for the wrong reasons, can bring great unhappiness to both partners. Although divorce is easier than ever before, it is always a painful and difficult option, and can be a deeply distressing and damaging experience for those involved – especially any children you might have.

Don't rush into marriage. If you have any lingering doubts, take time now to get to know your partner better, before finally making up your mind. Of course, many people have a few secret fears before they marry, and no one can guarantee what will happen in the future. Rather than hide those fears away however, and hope that they will disappear, it makes far more sense to examine them honestly and talk them over with your partner *before* you walk down the aisle.

A home of your own

Unless you are already living together, or unless one partner simply intends to move in with the other after the wedding, your first priority – along with arranging your wedding – will be finding a home.

If you are both earning low salaries, or intend to move to a different town in the fairly near future, you may decide to rent accommodation rather than attempt to buy. In this case you may have to take the best you can find, since rented accommodation can be hard to come by. You will almost certainly have to pay a deposit (which may be returnable when you leave), plus rent in advance.

Buying a house or flat is still an excellent investment if you can afford it. Your first step should be to shop around for the best mortgage deal you can find. Visit your local building society or bank, taking details of your salaries with you, and they will be able to estimate how much you would be entitled to borrow, and tell you the cost of repayments. Other lenders include local authorities and insurance companies. Some large building firms offer special schemes on starter homes on their estates. A mortage broker can fix a loan for you – at no cost to you. Many lenders have favourable arrangements for first-time buyers, so it's worth trying several sources for a loan.

When working out your finances, as well as calculating your mortgage repayments, there is a whole string of other costs to be taken into account. If you do not have much money saved, it might be possible to arrange a bank loan to cover some of these expenses.

Deposit   You may not be able to borrow the full amount to cover the cost of the property you want to buy, in which case you will have to put down a deposit of 10% or more when contracts are exchanged.

Solicitor's fees   Ask for an estimate of conveyancing costs when you brief your solicitor. These will be based partly on the cost of the property, with additional charges for making local authority searches, registering the property transfer, plus any other services such as extra correspondence, etc. Remember that if there are any legal hitches along the way, the solicitor's fee will go up.

Stamp duty   Currently 1% of the purchase price on properties costing over £30,000. This will be billed to you by your solicitor.

Your lender's legal and valuation fees   Ask for an estimate of these when discussing your loan.

Survey costs   The cheapest type of survey is a mortgage report and valuation, which is usually carried out by the lender. If you want something more detailed, ask for a RICS (Royal Institute of Chartered Surveyors) report and valuation. However, if you are buying a house or flat that is more than about 20 years old, it is best to have a full structural survey, which will be more expensive but could save you a lot of money in the long run. The cost of any survey will be related to the price of the property.

Building insurance   Usually arranged by the lender, with an annual premium to be paid by you.

Contents insurance   Your lender may be able to arrange this for you as well, but it could be worthwhile getting quotes from one or two other companies before you arrange the policy. The cost will depend on the insurer's assessment of the burglary risk in the area where the property is situated.

Life insurance   If you have an endowment mortgage, the monthly life insurance premium will be quoted as part of the mortgage repayment. On other types of mortgage, you will need a mortgage protection life policy. Again, your lender should be able to advise on this.

Selling a property   If either of you has a property to sell, you will have to pay estate agent's fees, usually around 2% of the value.

Any work needed on the property   Essential work, such as repairs to the roof or treatment for woodworm or rot, may be required by your lender before the full loan is advanced. You should be able to budget to do other, less urgent repairs, over a period of some months after you move in.

Decorating Although you can save a lot of money by doing this yourselves, don't set too ambitious a programme, especially if you are both working full-time. Work on one room at a time, and make it a priority to get at least one room comfortable as soon as possible so that you have somewhere to retreat.

Furnishing and carpeting Wedding gifts may take care of some of these items. You can furnish cheaply from large chainstores, or you might enjoy scouring local junk shops and auction rooms for secondhand bargains.

Removal costs For a small amount of furniture and belongings you will probably be able to hire a van and move yourselves. If either of you owns a lot of furniture or any valuable and fragile item, such as a piano, it is worth paying experts to move it for you.

Costs for flat-dwellers If you are buying a flat, enquire about the ground rent. There may also be substantial regular bills for service charges and you may be responsible for a share in the cost of repairs to the whole building, not just your flat.

Regular bills Once you move into your new home you will be liable for the local community charge and water rates. And you'll also have to budget for regular bills of course, including gas, electricity and telephone.

House hunting

Once you've worked out how much you can afford to spend, you can start looking at properties. When deciding where to look, consider property prices in a particular area, as well as the ease and cost of travelling to and from work, the proximity of shops and parks and, if you plan to start a family in your first home, nurseries and schools. Having chosen an area, ask local agents to put you on their mailing list.

Decide how many rooms you would like ideally: how

many bedrooms do you need, can you manage with one living room, rather than a separate sitting and dining room, are you desperate to have a garden or a garage, or to live away from the noise of traffic? You're unlikely to find a property that meets all your criteria, but at least your list will give you a starting point.

Look at lots of properties and remember that decoration can be changed: the important thing is to check how sound the structure of the house or flat is, so inspect window frames, brick pointing, the roof and chimneys for signs of decay or damage. Ask if the house has a damp course and has been treated for woodworm or dry rot. Check out the heating system and ask the occupiers how much it costs to run. Find out exactly which fixtures and fittings such as spotlights, built-in cookers, shelving, fitted carpets, curtains, etc are included in the price.

Allow plenty of time to buy your new home and move in. Unless you are lucky enough to find a house with vacant possession, it is likely to be around three months from the time your offer is accepted before you can move in – and that assumes that your sellers' move also goes ahead on schedule.

One final point: make sure that the deeds of the property are drawn up in your joint names. This is a common-sense safeguard to ensure that in the event of a future separation, both partners would have a legal entitlement to a share in the house. Ask your solicitor for further advice on this.

Money matters

How best to arrange your finances after you are married calls for diplomatic discussion. A lot will depend on how you both feel about money, and whether you have similar attitudes to saving and spending. Many couples are hard up in the early days of marriage but this only becomes a problem if they can't agree on their spending priorities, or if one feels that the other is overspending on non-essential items. These basic differences in attitude can be difficult to sort out and couples who know they have different attitudes to money should make allowance for this and think very carefully before deciding to pool their resources so that both partners have access to all joint funds.

There's no need to have any very complicated arrangements, but many people find it useful to run more than one bank or savings account. Some of the possibilities are listed here:

Joint accounts The simplest – but not necessarily the best – solution is to have one joint bank account only, into which both earnings go and from which all expenses are paid. This may be unfair, however, if one of you is earning much more than the other, and may also deprive you of the freedom to spend at least some of your money entirely as you wish, without consulting your partner.

Joint account plus personal accounts Perhaps a better way to organise your finances is to open a joint bank account from which regular household expenses are paid. You then estimate your monthly expenditure and agree what proportion you will both contribute: this could be a simple 50/50 split, or something different, depending on your earnings. Each partner pays an agreed amount each month into the joint account and at the same time retains a personal account for their own spending.

Keeping a kitty It can be useful to keep a small cash 'kitty' which you both keep 'topped up' when necessary, and from which you pay for small items of day to day shopping. Or you might decide to keep a note of what you spend on minor household expenses and settle up once a week.

Bills You can pay them from a joint account to which you've contributed an agreed proportion. Some couples prefer to take it in turns to pay, or agree that each will be wholly responsible for certain regular bills.

Savings You might want to pool all your 'spare' money into a joint savings account, or you could contribute an agreed monthly amount to joint savings, and save separately as and when you are able to if you wish. How the jointly saved money is then spent is up for discussion.

121

Credit cards A joint credit card account can be useful for staggering payments on large items, as long as you trust each other not to run up huge bills. Some couples also keep separate accounts for their personal expenses.

One task which is frequently ignored, but which should be done as soon as you are married, is that of making a will. A solicitor can advise you and, assuming the bequests are straightforward, the cost should not be too high. Marriage invalidates any previous wills, so this must be done by both of you as soon as possible after the wedding. Don't think that making a will is unnecessary because you plan to leave everything to each other. The property of a person who dies without making a will can be inaccessible for many months, while the estate goes through probate, causing considerable anguish and possible hardship to those left behind. Remember to update your wills occasionally as your circumstances change: on the birth of a child, perhaps, or when you move house.

Adjusting to marriage

A good marriage is endlessly rewarding, but it is a relationship with a life of its own, and is never static. It grows as the partners grow, and develops with them. It is seldom easy, but it is always rewarding, and the more you both put into it, the more you will get back. However, it can take a while to get used to the reality of married life, and loving each other is only half the story – you have to learn to live with each other as well.

One change you may not have bargained for is your change in identity. Married couples tend to be treated as a 'unit' – fine, for much of the time, but there's no need to think that you can't, or shouldn't, see friends alone or keep up your interests and hobbies without always including your partner. Of course, some couples are happy to do everything together, while others spend several evenings a week pursuing separate interests. Just how much independence and freedom you need and want is something for each individual to decide, and for each couple to agree on.

You may find too that you have less privacy than you had before marriage, especially if you are living in a small flat. Some people are not too bothered by this, but others hanker for some time and space to themselves. Needing time alone is not a rejection of your partner, but an expression of your real needs as an individual, so talk over how you feel and try to find a way in which you can have a bit of 'time off' to yourself, now and then.

What's in a name?

Married women take on a new identity if, as most do, they change to their husband's surname. For some, becoming 'Mrs' is a great pleasure, and they can relinquish their old name with no regrets. Others find it quite a shock to suddenly be addressed as 'Mrs John Smith', and feel that they have lost something in giving up their maiden name. Some women adopt the solution of retaining their maiden name at work and using their married name in private life. However, do remember that some government departments (eg HM Inspector of Taxes, National Insurance, etc) will need to know your married name.

Domestic details

If both partners are working, they will have to take some decisions about responsibility for running the household. Whose job is it to do the washing and ironing, the shopping, cooking, and cleaning, and to deal with domestic paperwork? Division of labour is the fairest answer, and the details will probably have to be thrashed out as you go along, but it pays to set the ground rules early on. If one partner gets used to being 'looked after' by the other, it could be very hard to make a change later.

Your sex life, too, may alter once you are living together permanently. Running a home may leave you feeling very tired – but on the other hand, perhaps now you have time and privacy together which were lacking before. You'll need to be sympathetic and understanding of each other's needs.

Long term planning

When you are making decisions about your future, look to the long term as well as the first year or so. What are your career plans? Does the woman have certain career goals to achieve before she has children? Do you both want children, and are you agreed about the timing, about who should bear the main responsibility for childcare, and about whether the woman will carry on working after the children are born?

Are there things you want to do together before you restrict your movements with young children? Do you long to travel, for instance? You might be happier postponing a family for a few years and saving for one or two good holidays first.

When you are making long term plans, remember your own parents. Sometimes, of course, a move away from home town and family is unavoidable for at least one partner. But it's sensible to include in the equation your parents' likely future needs and look at ways in which you might cope with these.

Although it's impossible to plan for all eventualities, it does make sense to examine these questions at the start of your married life and make the first move towards finding the answers that will emerge during the years to come.

Index